Book Marketing

SUCCESS

101 Ways to Promote Your Book

BY

AMELIA GRIGGS

Identifiers:

ISBN: 978-1-7372096-0-7

Published by Green Ridge Press

Green Ridge Press

Cover design by Debbie O'Byrne, JetLaunch

Your voice matters, and without it, we don't exist.

Please support us and leave a review!

Table of Contents

Dedication

To every writer in the world.

Remember that your books make a difference.

Thank You and Gratitude

To my family, for your patience and understanding.

About This Book

You have written a book and now it is published and available for the world to see – or so you thought. Perhaps it is an eBook, a paperback, or a hardcover book. You have spent months or even years on your book. Now it's time to get ready to do the real work: marketing.

One thing is for certain: your book will not sell itself. Initially, your book may sell a few copies or even dozens of copies. However, if you are an unknown author, and if the genre of your book is too saturated, there's a pretty good chance that your book will get lost in the sea of millions of other books. To prevent this from happening, and to ensure that your book not only sells some copies initially, but keeps on selling, it is important to consider using a variety of marketing strategies to promote your book. It is also about identifying and connecting with your audience and finding people who *want* to buy your book.

In this book, you will learn 101 ways to promote your book, including no cost and low-cost marketing strategies. Also included are more costly marketing methods to consider, some dos and don'ts, and additional marketing tips.

There is a lot of material covered, and in some cases, there are links to articles and videos I have put together to further demonstrate processes and techniques.

Whether you are new to marketing, or if you have already started promoting your book and need help moving forward, this book can help you get there. Feel free to browse through the table of contents to select specific topics to help you along your book marketing journey.

"The secret of getting ahead is getting started."

~Mark Twain

The purpose of this book is to help you find the best ways to *successfully* market your book. The amount of marketing and promoting you pursue is entirely up to you. Marketing results will vary for each person, and for each book. The more strategies you attempt, the better the likelihood that you will discover the methods which work best for your book. This book is not meant to overwhelm you – instead, it's designed to help you be more aware of the many marketing options, and help you pick and choose strategies as you continue along your marketing journey.

In some cases, I refer to marketing tools on Amazon or Kindle Direct Publishing (KDP). If you don't use KDP for publishing, there are still dozens of marketing strategies you can use throughout this book.

Like my other books and materials in the Author Journey Success Toolkit series, this book is based on my experience of marketing and promoting books in various genres. This includes strategies on how to pre-market your book, how to create book mockup graphics, how to get honest reviews, how to get involved in book launch and author events, how to optimize metadata for your book, and a whole lot more. It also includes guidance on having the right marketing mindset, as well as things not to do.

Also included is honest information about the costs involved when pursuing marketing strategies. Although there are a variety of no-cost methods you can try to promote your book, there are also low-cost methods and more expensive ways to market books.

So, grab a drink and a snack and get ready to discover a boatload of ways to market your book. Some methods are fun and easy while some take a bit more work. You can choose which marketing strategies are a good fit for you and for your book.

You can read this book in its entirety or skip around as you see fit. Remember to bookmark sections to help you refer to during your marketing journey.

Now, let the book marketing begin!

Getting Started

#1

Define Your Ideal Customer

Before you start marketing, there's one important thing you must do (if you didn't do it already): identify your audience. Be sure to determine and know your audience including age, genre, and gender. You can't effectively market to your readers if you don't know who you are readers are.

#2

Define Your Marketing Goals

What is your goal in marketing your book? You might not think of setting goals as a marketing strategy, but it is important to define some realistic marketing goals when it comes to selling a book. Even if you try every single strategy in this book, if you haven't set marketing goals, how will you measure the level of success for your book sales?

What are your goals as an author? What is important to you most: the number of reviews, the number of sales, or popularity?

What is your marketing budget? Are you willing to spend some money on advertising and promotional materials?

How much do you want to earn as an author?

Defining marketing goals doesn't have to be complicated. It can be as simple as deciding that you want to earn $50/month, $200/month, or $1000/month in royalties. Of course, the more money you want to earn, the more book sales you will need. I'm going to suggest that you start small and then grow from there. Just like Rome wasn't built in a day, the same is true for your marketing strategies. It will take time to experiment with different types of marketing, and gradually, you will discover what works best for *you*, to promote your book.

Consider a short-term goal and a long-term goal. For example, perhaps you wrote a historical fiction romance novel, and you are hoping it becomes a movie someday. In the interim, a short-term goal would be to achieve the bestseller banner on Amazon within 3 months and be interviewed by a local radio show about your book. Your short-term royalty goal might be that you want to earn at least $50/month for the first quarter, increasing to $100/month in the next quarter, and so forth. Over the course of 2 years, you decide you want to earn enough money to hire a script writer and business coach to move towards your long-term goal to turn your book into a movie.

Let's look at another example. Let's say you wrote a nonfiction book that solves a common problem. You already have people interested in your book and you decide to create several more books and create a series within the next 2 years. In the short-term, you want to earn enough to work part-time within 1 year. As a long-term goal, you want to earn enough income with book sales so you can resign from your current job within 3 years.

Some authors just want to write a book for the sheer joy of seeing their writing in print. If you are writing a series of love poems to your sweetheart and you decide to publish the book just for fun, the outcome will be successful because the joy of holding a book with your special poems which you wrote from the heart is all you need.

For the time being, write down at least one short-term goal and one long-term goal for your book. Revisit your goals in 3, 6 and 12 months.

If you are not where you want to be and not earning enough royalty, then you may need to adjust your goals, your marketing strategies, or both.

Pre-Marketing

Ideally, pre-marketing should be done *before* you launch your book. If you haven't launched your book just yet, you can use the methods in this section to get started with pre-marketing. If your book is already live and launched, no worries – you can still use these strategies to re-release your book. This is comparable to stores and shops having a grand re-opening. Consider using the same strategy as part of a grand re-release for your book! Even if your book has been around for some time, consider resurrecting it and breathing new life into it. It's never too late to re-market a book.

Most pre-marketing strategies can also be used ongoing to promote your book!

#3

Book Launch Announcements
Create online book announcement posts ahead of time. Start with something simple. Compose several announcements to post online at different time intervals to announce your book. Post your announcements on social media wherever you have the most followers. The cost is free. Here are some post ideas:

Post #1 – Create a *"Coming Soon on MM/DD/YYYY"* and include one or two statements about your book. If it is nonfiction, what problem does it solve? If it is fiction, include a short synopsis but consider including a cliff hanger.

Post #2 – Do a book cover reveal. Show your cover for an added teaser and add the words *"Cover Reveal"* in a starburst shape. See the *Book Mockups* section to learn how to create book mockups to use as promotional graphics.

Post #3 – Include a lengthier synopsis with reasons why your book is unique. Include a countdown statement like *"10 Days to Go!"* to build suspense.

Post #4 – Post an announcement on your launch day or re-release day. Make it fun and exciting. Include a picture of yourself holding your book. Remember to include a link where they can buy your book.

#4

Select an Email Marketing Service

Prior to your official book launch or re-release, spend some time evaluating different email marketing services such as MailChimp, AWeber, Constant Contact, ConvertKit, and so forth. A good email marketing service should:

- Allow you to create highly engaging email newsletters.
- Provide an easy-to-use interface with drag-and-drop editing functions.
- Allow you to send bulk emails that are personalized.
- Provide helpful statistics for tracking and monitoring.
- Contain easy marketing campaigns to set up.
- Allow you to easily manage your contact list, including the use of tags for separating your list into groups.

Email marketing services vary with regards to cost and functionality. Some are initially free, up to a certain number of subscribers; then there is a monthly fee based on subscriber count. I started out with MailChimp since it was free to use with up to 2K subscribers. At the time of writing this book, Mailerlite and ConvertKit both have free plans up to 1K subscribers, and Aweber is free for up to 500 subscribers. Constant Contact doesn't have a free plan, but they do have a 30-day free trial; then it's $20/month for up to 500 subscribers. See the *Resources* section in the back of this book for links to pricing.

Building your list is equally important before, during and after your book launch. When composing an email to potential customers, how do you build your email list? The easiest way is to offer helpful information for free. The free content can be included in your email or in a link to download a file. Here are a few ideas:

- If your book is about cooking, offer a free recipe from your book.
- If your book is about technology, offer a list of tech tips.
- If your book is a novel, include a lengthy synopsis from chapter 1.
- For a children's picture book, include several pages from inside the book.

#5

Build Your Brand

If your background is horticulture, and you decide to write a book about gardening, there is a higher chance that your potential audience will trust that you are experienced in that field, and they may be more inclined to buy your book.

On the other hand, if you are an archeologist who secretly loves to dance and you decide to write a book on ballroom dancing, your potential audience might be a little confused. In any case, no matter what you write about, it's pertinent that you build your brand. Consider establishing a connection between you and your book.

My Own Case Study: With a background in IT Training and Instructional Design, I knew if I wrote a romance novel, that would be a bit more risqué, and more challenging to market due to my time constraints. When I first got serious about writing a book, I was working full-time with a full plate of everything under the sun, and although I like to think *big*, I knew I had to be realistic. So, I decided to start with a smaller experiment and build from there – I began with a technology series. I knew if I started with something more up my alley, I would be able to market it. Don't worry if you cannot connect your career with your book. It doesn't always make sense, especially if you are writing fiction. In this case, build your brand like you are starting a new career – treat it like a new business venture.

Here are some ideas on how you can build your brand and help potential readers learn more about *you*:

- **Think of your writing as a business**. Create a logo for your book business and add it to your email signature, and on social media posts. Consider adding your logo to your book cover as well. If it's not ideal to add your logo to the front cover, consider adding it to the back cover, or somewhere inside the book.
- **Book a photo shoot**. Prepare some headshot images including one of you holding your book. Find a local photographer or ask a friend to take some pictures of you with good lighting. Don't use a selfie which may tend to look unprofessional.

- **Record and share a video**. Discuss why you love to write, what your book is about, and how you came up with the idea for your book.
- **Engage with your audience**. Ask questions using an online poll to learn more about what your potential audience wants to read and how you can help them (nonfiction) or entertain them (fiction). Know your audience!
- **Build an author platform.** Before you release your book, it is important to market yourself and provide value to the public. However, don't just talk about your book and yourself; tell readers why they might like the book, what the book is about, and how it can help them in some way.

As far as the costs of building your brand, this depends on your budget and your ability to create your own materials vs. hiring someone else.

For logos, there are several free tools available including logomaker.com, Shopify's free logo maker (Hatchful), and Canva. All these tools have a variety of logo templates. See the *Resources* section in the back of this book for website information on logos and marketing materials.

Note: For Canva, you can start with the free version or upgrade to Canva Pro if you need more images and templates. I have been using Canva Pro for several years and it is well worth the cost of $12.99/month, which includes 100+ million photos, videos, and media; it also includes over 600,000 templates.

For business cards, I typically use Vista Print, but more recently, I have been using Canva to create most of my marketing materials.

For a professional head shot, photo studios are not always the best solution. In the past, I purchased a $100 package at a nearby photo studio; the backdrops were limited, and the outcome was average quality. More recently, I used a cropped image of myself from an outdoor family event for my signature social media photo; I used a free app for minor touchups. Overall, the amateur photo turned out better and it was free!

#6

Pre-Order Giveaways

Before your book is even live and available, it's important to create some buzz. If your book is already live, a giveaway strategy will still work anytime. I know an author who did a giveaway with 30 prizes! Although you can consider giving away signed copies of your book, you don't have to necessarily give your book away. Instead, consider creating some gift baskets with some book themed merchandise such as bookmarks, postcards, or other author's books. This does require a small investment to purchase some giveaway items. As an alternative, you can give away digital products such as free chapters so there is no cost involved. Remember to include information on how they can purchase your book!

#7

Book Mockups

As soon as you have your book cover ready, it's time to create some book mockups! When creating marketing graphics, showing a flat image of your book cover is certainly acceptable, but seeing a 3D image of your book is a bit more captivating. I have experimented with various tools to create book mockups, which I have listed below. There seems to be a lot more rectangular book mockup choices vs. square book sizes. For my first series, I used 7" X 10" for my trim size. In addition, I created a Large Print version for one of my books with an 8" X 10" trim size. Although I did find some free mockup tools that worked, the mockup image didn't always fit the bill. In some cases, the book cover image must be a certain size. At times, you can crop the image slightly to fit; in other cases, it's a matter of trial and error to determine what mockup template will work best with your book cover.

For my children's rhyming series, I used a trim size of 8 ½" X 8 ½". This square trim size is quite popular with children's books and fits well in some social media platforms like Instagram, which uses square vs. rectangular images. However, for mockups, this proved to be a bit more challenging since the tools I tried had a lot more choices for rectangular vs. square images.

As an alternative to creating your own mockups, you can consider hiring someone to create mockup images for you. When I couldn't find the square size I needed for my children's book mockups, I hired someone on Fiverr and the price was reasonable. If you do hire someone to create mockup graphics, be sure to ask for a set of images with a transparent background saved to PNG file format. This will allow you to overlay the mockup on any background you like. Here are some 3D mockup tools that I've tried:

Placeit.net – One mockup tool I use is placeit.net. They have a variety of book mockups, as well as many other types of mockups for other products. They have a free account as well as monthly/yearly subscription options. The monthly fee is $14.95, or you can pay $86.69 for the year which equates to $7.47/month, and you save 50%.

Creative Indie Covers – Another tool to try is Derek Murphy's free book mockup tool. This is a good tool to try if you are just starting out, and if your trim size is rectangular vs. square. The link is **https://www.creativindiecovers.com/free-online-3d-book-cover-generator.**

Covervault.com – Mockups on this website come in a variety of sizes and backgrounds, and they are free to download. However, files are in PSD (Photoshop Document) format, so you either need to have Adobe Photoshop or another tool which allows you to edit PSD files. Unless you are familiar with how to edit PSD files, this option can be time consuming and more confusing than the other tools.

#8

Alternatives to 3D Mockups

As an alternative to 3D mockups, flat images of your book cover with an attractive background and the right graphics can work out nicely. I love using Canva to combine graphics for social media posts, marketing graphics and announcements. They have a variety of templates, many of which are free. If you don't have Canva Pro, you can purchase individual templates, but you will need to purchase them separately. If you end up purchasing a lot of media, upgrading to Canva Pro is more cost-effective.

BONUS: Mockup Examples

Below are just a few examples of book mockups, including flat graphics and 3D graphics. I have indicated what tool I have used to create each graphic.

The image below is a pre-launch graphic I created using Snagit. In this image, I used a background I purchased, and I added additional text overlayed on semi-transparent shapes. The 3D mockup image of the front and back book cover was an image created from someone I hired on Fiverr.

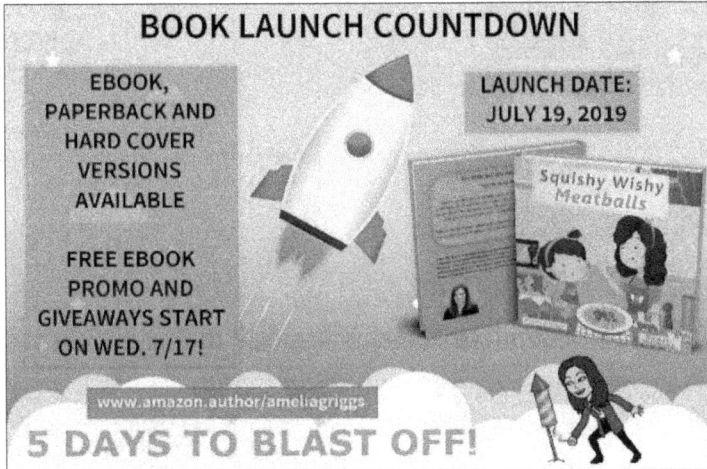

Children's Books Promotional Graphics – Created in Canva (using template size for Instagram, which is also suitable for Facebook posts):

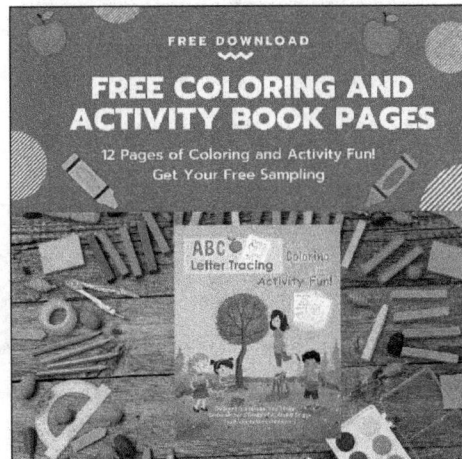

Nonfiction Books Promotional Graphics – Created in Canva (the 3D book mockup graphics included in the images were created by my book designer, JetLaunch, who I hired to create the book covers for this series):

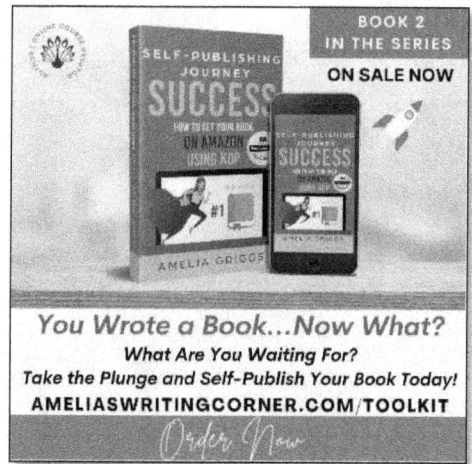

Nonfiction Books Promotional Graphics – Created in Placeit.net:

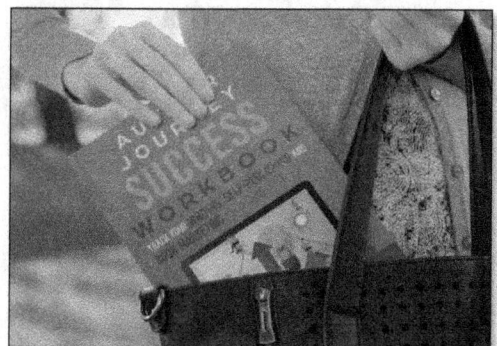

Facebook banner using flat images of book covers - Created in Canva (the bookshelf background was duplicated several times and rotated horizontally to give the appearance of a large bookshelf area):

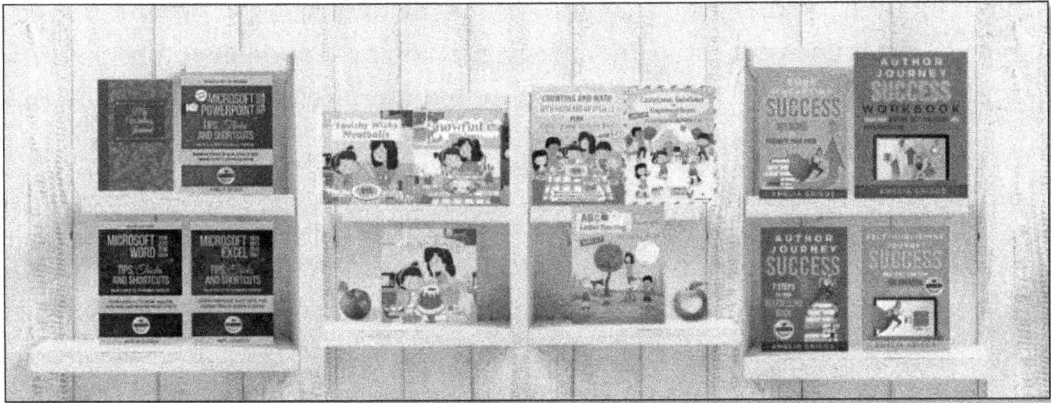

#9

How to Get Honest Reviews

Book reviews can be in the form of testimonials, social media feedback, or official Amazon reviews. For testimonials, reviewers typically send you the wording electronically for you to use in your marketing materials. If you receive feedback about your book on social media, it is probably best to ask the person who posted it for permission to use their name and comments as a testimonial.

If you are planning on selling most of your books via Amazon, it's important to get as many reviews as possible posted on Amazon. As a goal, try to get at least 10 reviews when you first release your book. This is sometimes like pulling teeth, but it's not impossible. Here are two free, easy ways to get reviews:

- Build a list of advanced readers.
- Including a note in the back of the book asking customers to post a review.

If you have an eBook version of your book, readers also have an opportunity to leave a star rating when they reach the end of your book.

Did you know that there are two types of reviews on Amazon? This includes *Ratings* and *Reviews*. *Ratings* are just star ratings, whereas *Reviews* contain commentary. Amazon introduced one-tap star ratings for product reviews in late 2019, which allow customers to provide a star rating without any commentary. The star rating shows as one of the ratings under Amazon reviews, but it does not show an Amazon customer name or any other information. These star ratings still help tremendously along with book reviews.

There are several ways to leave a star rating, or an official review with commentary:

- If customers purchase your book directly from Amazon, they can go to the *Write a Product Review* page for your book from their *Amazon Orders* page. If they did not purchase your book directly from Amazon, they can click *Write a Customer Review* which can be found by scrolling down towards the bottom left of your book listing page; next, from the *Create a Review* page, if they only want to leave a star rating, they can *just* click the number of stars to rate the book; at that point, a green checkmark confirms the submission and they can exit from the review page without leaving any commentary and the star rating is recorded. However, if they want to add commentary, they can continue filling out the information on the review page including the *Headline*, and *Written Review comments;* and then they would click *Submit*.
- For eBooks, customers can click on the number of stars to rate a book when they reach the end of the book on Kindle.

If someone purchases your book from Amazon and leaves a review with commentary, their review will contain the words *Verified Purchase*. This means that the item was purchased directly from Amazon. Their account must also meet certain requirements to post a review. For example, at the time of writing this book, Amazon requires that a customer has spent at least $50.00 on Amazon in the past year.

There will be plenty of times that customers purchase your book outside of Amazon. They may purchase it from another website, from a bookstore, or in person at a book event. Readers may also receive a free copy of your book via a giveaway event or if they are an advanced reader. You can learn more about advanced readers in the next section, the *ARC Strategy*. If someone does not purchase your book on Amazon, they can still post a review on Amazon, but the words *Verified Purchase* do not show above their review. This is perfectly fine and will still count as a review. However, it's most helpful to have at least some reviews from customers who purchased your book directly from Amazon. Verified purchase reviews rank higher than unverified reviews, since there is less concern about potential issues associated with unverified reviews. The quantity and quality of reviews can increase your book's visibility on search pages.

If you are wondering if you should hire people to review your book and post a review, here is my advice: *Never pay for reviews!* Here's why:

- It's not good practice and Amazon frowns upon this method. The best reviews are from customers who are truly interested in reading your book. Although they may not all be positive, they will be honest.
- There are hundreds, if not thousands of websites which will gladly take your money to post a review. Be very careful of these websites, especially ones who rate books in all genres. Since the reviewers are paid to post a review, do you think they care one iota about your book? Probably not. Of course, there are exceptions. I have seen websites where people offer free reviews, but they require you to sign up, provide your email address, and email them an electronic copy of your book.
- There is no guarantee that paid reviewers will post a positive review, so in the long run, you may be paying for a review that is not in good taste.

Other ways to get reviews:

Run a KDP Select Free Promo Deal. If you are using KDP for publishing your book, KDP Select is free and allows you to price your eBook for FREE for up to 5 days in each enrollment period (90 days, for example). Any reviews posted by customers who purchase your free eBook is counted as a verified purchase. Remember to promote your free eBook day(s) and include a reminder for takers to please post a review.

Build Your Email List and Send a Free Copy. Consider sending interested subscribers a note about your book and why they might be interested in reading it. You can even offer to send them a free physical copy by using the gift option on Amazon; then after a few weeks, ask, but don't beg, for a review. *Note*: The Amazon gift option may only be available within your country.

Welcome Testimonials. Even though testimonials are not as valuable as an official online review, you can add testimonials to your website, blog and even below your book description on Amazon. Some readers are not comfortable posting an online review, but they may be willing to send you a few sentences you can use for a testimonial.

Ask For a Review Inside Your Book. Inside your book, add a note asking for feedback and a review. I like to include a note in the back of the book asking readers if they liked the book and if they can post a review. I also include instructions on how to post a review. You can use the instructions at the beginning of this section to include in your note for readers. The more options you give them, the better. More recently, I also include a short note at the bottom of the copyright page that reads:

Your voice matters, and without it, we don't exist.

Please support us and leave a review!

What To Do If You Get Negative Reviews:

We all want positive feedback, but it's important to be open to receiving any type of feedback, including critical feedback and negative comments. Even bestselling books have some bad reviews. If it is honest feedback, it may help to improve your book. If it's purely negative feedback, turn it into a positive. For example, for one of my books, someone posted a short but not so sweet review with 1 star. The review comment says *Don't buy it.* At first, I was saddened and angry that someone would post such a comment, but in the end, I realized that was just someone's opinion. Also, because 95% of the comments for my book were positive, the consensus was that readers liked the book and found it helpful. Don't let negative comments or reviews bring you down. Instead, rise about them and move forward.

If you receive a negative review which you feel is unfair or unacceptable, contact KDP and ask them if they would consider removing the review.

The ARC Strategy

The ARC, or Advanced Reader Copy strategy can be used to share your manuscript with interested readers ahead of time, to try and get advanced feedback, early testimonials, and reviews. The goal is to have 10 reviews during launch week to boost the ranking of your book. Here's how it works:

1. At least 4 weeks (or more) prior to your book release, send a PDF copy of your manuscript to a list of advanced readers. If you don't have a list just yet, start building one now. If your goal is to get 10 reviews, plan to contact at least 40 to 50 readers. If you want to try to get 25 reviews, reach out to 100 readers. Not everyone will review your book. Remember to spend some time crafting a pitch letter which includes a summary of your book, some reasons why they may want to read it, and how you would like to offer them a free copy.

2. Approximately, 2 weeks later, send a follow-up reminder to the advanced readers to remind them to review your book. When your readers provide feedback to you about your book, it may be:
   a. An acknowledgement that they have read your book (this may require a 2nd of 3rd nudge email on your part).
   b. Some honest feedback to help you with improvements to your book (example: Suzie lets you know that she has read your book and found 2 grammar errors).
   c. A promise that they will leave you a review on Amazon when your book launches (example: John texts you that he has read the advanced copy and he can't wait until your book launches so he can post a review on Amazon).
   d. A testimonial which you can use and apply to your book's back cover, the inside of your book, or on promotional materials.
   e. A review which the reader would like to post on Amazon as a verified purchase. Some advanced readers truly want to purchase your book whether it is free or not free.

3. When your book is live on Amazon, providing you are enrolled in KDP Select, run a free promo deal for your eBook for one day or several days; tell your ARC team ahead of time about your free promo deal. Ask your advanced readers to purchase your eBook for free on Amazon

during your promotion. Hopefully, they have already read your book by now since you sent them an advanced copy weeks prior. Prompt them to post a review on Amazon, and since they purchased a free copy, it will contain the *Verified Purchase* heading above their review.

If you have a large following already for a related product or publication, you can leverage what you have – send an email to each of your followers, let them know that you have written a book, and ask them if they would be interested in reading it ahead of your launch and provide you with honest feedback.

If you don't have a following yet, not to worry – you can start small and build from there. Prepare something you can give away for free, preferably something electronic, such as an information sheet about your book, a free chapter, a book trailer, or a synopsis with a cliff hanger. The idea is to prepare some interesting bait, go fishing and reel your followers in! It would be best to invest in an email marketing program like MailChimp, Aweber, etc. to help you setup a landing page with your freebie offer. This will be in the form of a link that you will then want to share everywhere, on Facebook, Instagram, LinkedIn, or whatever platform you are the most active.

As an alternative, you can visit *https://www.amazon.com/review/top-reviewers* to look through Amazon's top book reviewers. With a little research, you can connect with top reviewers and ask them if they are interested in reviewing your book. Consider reviewers who have reviewed similar books in your genre. Reviews from top reviewers is *gold*! I tried this and it is time consuming but worth a try; maybe try to contact a dozen reviewers and see if any respond. If their contact information is not available, try googling their name to find them on social media. Here is a sample message when asking a top reviewer to review your book:

Hello,

I know you are busy, so I will make this brief. After reviewing your profile on Amazon, I noticed you are interested in [insert book subject here] and the good news is that I just finished writing a book on that subject. I would like to send you an advanced copy and would love it if you could leave a brief review when you have time. I look forward to hearing from you.

Thanks in advance.

[Your name]
[Your contact information]

KDP, KDP Select and Price Promotions

KDP offers a free promotional tool for eBooks called KDP Select. You can sign up for KDP Select in the *Bookshelf* section of your KDP dashboard. Once enrolled, you can setup a Kindle Countdown Deal or a Free Book Promotion.

While enrolled in KDP Select, you are also automatically enrolled in the Kindle Unlimited (KU) program, which can potentially increase your royalties. This depends on the number of pages read for your book. KU allows customers to read as many eBooks as they like for a monthly subscription fee.

To enroll in KDP Select, you must have exclusive rights for the primary content of your eBook (i.e., the content cannot be public domain). You must also agree to make your eBook exclusive to the Kindle Store for the KDP Select enrollment period which is currently 90-days. Enrollment renewal is usually automatic; therefore, if you decide that KDP Select is not for you, you may need to uncheck the auto renewal checkbox. *Note*: If you are planning on selling your book elsewhere, then you will need to opt out of KDP Select.

#11

Run a Kindle Countdown Deal (KDP)

When and why should you increase or decrease the price of your book? If your book is selling like hotcakes, then do not decrease the price. If anything, consider increasing the price slightly to earn more royalties. On the other hand, if your book is not selling well and needs a boost, consider decreasing the price for a few days in the form of a sale. You can change the price manually as needed; or, if you are enrolled in KDP Select, consider running a countdown deal. A Kindle Countdown deal allows you to sell your book at a lower starting price on a particular date, then gradually returns to the retail price.

#12

Run a Free Promo Deal (KDP)

Why should you consider one or more free promo days and give your eBook away for free using KDP Select or any other free promo service? To cause a spike in sales! During the first 30 days when your book goes live, the more activity and more book sales, the higher the chance that you will achieve the #1 New Release banner on Amazon. Higher sales coupled with selecting the best categories and using the right metadata may also help you achieve the #1 Bestselling Banner as well! KDP Select's Promo Free Book Promotion allows you to sell your eBook for free for up to 5 days. Amazon loves books that do well during the first 30 days, and they will keep promoting your book beyond 30 days if your activity and sales continue to increase.

To learn more about KDP Select, I've included step-by-step instructions and screen prints in the following article: *https://toughnickel.com/self-employment/How-to-Create-a-Kindle-Countdown-Deal-for-your-Amazon-KDP-eBooks*.

#13

Perma-Free Books

Another strategy to consider is the perma-free eBook. A permanently free eBook, or *perma-free* book is used to lure potential customers to your main book, or a book series. If you are planning to write a book series, you can offer the first eBook for free to get readers interested in your series. If you are selling a course or other product, a perma-free eBook can act as your lead magnet.

On KDP, the lowest price you can set for your eBook is .99 cents, and since KDP Select only allows you to sell your eBook for free for up to 5 days during each enrollment period, how do you sell your eBook for free on Amazon? One option is to use Draft 2 Digital (D2D) or Smashwords to publish your eBook for free and then have KDP do a price match. After you publish your eBook on KDP, don't enroll in KDP Select. If you already enrolled in KDP Select, be sure to uncheck the auto enrollment box. When the enrollment period ends, publish your eBook on D2D or Smashwords and set the price to $0.00. If you make your book available in Smashwords' Premium catalog, your book is eligible for free syndication to Barnes and Noble, iBooks, and other websites. Next, let KDP support know that your book is available for free on another platforms, and ask them to a price match of $0 for your eBook on KDP. Be sure to include a link to one of the other platforms to KDP support for proof that your eBook is currently listed for free. *Note*: Both Smashwords and Draft 2 Digital are free publishing platforms.

#14

Seasonal Sales/Anniversary Sales

Similar to how brick and mortar businesses and online companies take advantage of the change of seasons, anniversaries and holidays for sales, consider running special promotions and deals at these times of the year as well. There is virtually no cost to do this if you create your own promotional graphics, which is easy to do in tools such as Canva.

Here are some ideas:

- End of summer celebration book sale: create a summer scene graphic.
- Pre-holiday sale: reduce the price a month before a holiday.
- Winter price reduction: include a note in your promotion graphic such as "Start the new year off to a great start!" for nonfiction, or "Curl up with a good book!" for fiction.
- Anniversary Sale: Create a celebratory promo graphic, include some testimonials, and list reasons why readers may love your book.

In Canva, you can search for the words, *book sale,* and find customizable graphics in a matter of minutes. To access all Canva templates, I would recommend Canva Pro. You can also sign up for a free 30-day trial.

To Canva Pro for free, visit: *https://geni.us/getcanva*

The next page includes sample graphics for seasonal sale events. They were created in Canva using pre-made templates.

30%
SUMMER
SALE
Limited time only

Up to 25% off!

SPRINGTIME SALE

May 1-10
In stores & online
www.123store.com

Winter
SALE
UP TO
50%
OFF

Book Events

Book events, whether online or in-person are very helpful in connecting with your audience. Of all the events I have attended, I have found in-person book festivals to be the most rewarding and pleasant experiences because:

- Meeting someone in person adds a special kind of value.
- You can chat with potential readers.
- You can ask people to pose with your book and take pictures, and with their permission, share the images on social media.
- Engagement is increased vs. just posting online.
- There are networking opportunities.
- Increase your email list (offer a freebie with sign-up sheet).
- Someone may ask you to speak at another event.
- You can talk to other authors for more ideas.

#15

Host An Online Book Event

Consider hosting a special event such as an online meet and greet, a video demonstration, or an author interview session. Plan an online event just like you would plan a party. Plan to post on social media prior to and on your special day with the graphics and strategies covered in the *Pre-Marketing* and *Book Mockup* sections covered earlier in this book. The cost of an online event should be fairly inexpensive.

Where you post may depend on which social media you are most active on, and what makes the most sense. Consider using a social media platform that offers event options. Facebook business pages allow you to create a live video, host an event, announce a job (this can be you announcing your new book business venture), create an offer, or run an ad. Personal Facebook pages allow you to create a live video, post a photo or video, or create a life event. Invite others and remember to give them a reason to join you and interact. This may include running a price promotion, posting a book trailer video, giving away a free chapter, or including a top 10 list about something related to your book.

#16

Do a Book Signing

Ideally, book signings should be in person. Start by contacting local book shops and inquire about doing a book signing. Don't limit yourself to just bookstores and local book shops. Depending on the genre for your book, consider other types of businesses as well. For example:

- If you wrote a children's book, consider ice cream shops or toy shops. Buy a few gift cards from the store and offer them as prizes if someone buys your book. This is a win-win situation for you and the local business.
- If you wrote a book on how to start a business, consider contacting your local community and township offices. Give away flyers with business tips.
- If you wrote a book on gardening, consider gardening centers or any place which sells flowers and gardening supplies. Buy a few gardening tools from the shop and make a gift basket to give away to visitors. You can collect their name and email address for entries, and this will help you build your email list.

#17

Sign-up for a Book Festival

Search online for local book festivals where you can sell your books. The cost of a book festival will range in price. Some festivals will provide a table, while some may only provide a space and require you to bring your own table. Consider investing in a folding table and outdoor tent. Decorate your table with bright colors, festive balloons, and signage.

For more helpful information to help you prepare for your in-person book fair or other book event, click here to learn 10 Things You Should Know About Your First Author Expo and Book Fair: *https://toughnickel.com/self-employment/10-Things-You-Should-Know-About-Your-First-Author-Expo-and-Book-Fair*.

#18

Contact Your Local Library

Reach out to local libraries and tell them you are a local author. Offer to donate a copy of your book so they can review it and consider purchasing some copies. Volunteer to host an event where you can do a book reading, activity or help the library in some way. Many local libraries also host yearly author events. Some author events at libraries are free, while others may charge a nominable fee.

#19

Do a Mini Book Tour

Carry a few copies of your books in a protective case in your car for impromptu visits. Anytime you visit a bookstore, library, garden center, gift shop, etc., look for an opportunity to show your books. Ask to speak to the manager, tell them you are a local author, and ask if they are interested in collaborating in some way, perhaps through a joint giveaway.

#20

Volunteer for a Speaking Event

If you are a subject matter expert in your field, consider volunteering to speak at a conference, fair or other book event. You can speak about your topic online, or in person, and let the audience know about your book at the end of your speech. This increases your exposure as an author, offers helpful information and gets the word out about your book. *Note*: If you wrote a children's book, contact local schools to inquire about doing a school visit.

Optimize Your Book

#21

Update Amazon Categories

If you are using KDP to publish your book, you can initially select two book categories. However, once your book is live on Amazon, you can add up to 10 categories. This is important to make your book more available when customers search in different categories. *Note*: Categories are different for eBooks and paperbacks.

To find relevant categories, go to amazon.com and select *Best Sellers* on the upper left. In the department menu, select *Books*. Then click on a genre. Make a list of relevant categories for your book; then contact KDP to request an update to your book's categories. To contact KDP, from the dashboard, click *Help*; then select *Contact Us* on the bottom left. From the *Amazon Store & Product Detail Page* section, click *Update Amazon Categories*.

#22

Track Your Book Rankings

Once your book is live on Amazon, it's a good idea to check the rankings for your book periodically. Rankings for your book may not display until there is ample sales activity for your book. Initially, you may want to monitor your book rankings daily. It's fun to watch book rankings, especially when your book is in the top 1000 or 100 ranking in a category.

To find book rankings on Amazon, go to your book listing on amazon.com, then scroll down to *Product Details*. Look at the section called *Best Seller's Rank*. Amazon displays the top 3 categories based on the book's activity and sales. Books in your genre with a ranking of less than #5000 may be an indication that the book is selling well, and/or it is getting a decent amount of search activity.

#23

Buy Some Copies of Your Book

Have you purchased any of your books lately? Once your book is live, you are free to purchase a few copies of your very own book, directly from Amazon! This will not only give your book a boost in sales and ranking, but it will also give you an opportunity to test out the process and earn royalty. If you need to purchase many copies of your paperback, you can also purchase author copies through KDP at a reduced rate; from the KDP bookshelf, click *Order Author Copies*. Using this method, you only pay for the cost of printing, plus the cost of shipping. However, you do not earn royalties when you purchase author copies.

#24

The #1 New Release Banner

Imagine the excitement and thrill of seeing the #1 New Release banner on your book listing on Amazon. If you play your cards right, you can also achieve the #1 Bestseller banner as well. Here are a few things you *must* know about these banners, including a few dirty little secrets:

- Amazon does not alert you if you achieve the #1 New Release Banner. That is why it is very important to check your book listing and ranking periodically to monitor the status of your book.
- Achieving the #1 New Release banner is very exciting. I will guarantee it will make you happy and smile. You may also get a euphoric feeling when you see it. That's exactly what happened to me, and it was certainly fun basking in the moment!
- You don't have to sell a million copies to get it.
- It can be deceiving – and your friends and family may assume this means you can quit your day job because you have become a millionaire.
- In my opinion, it is definitely something you want to aim to achieve. Even if it does not equate to big sales, it equates to reaching a huge milestone.

- The banner might not display for a long time. Amazon updates statistics hourly, so depending on your activity and sales, the banner may be here today and gone tomorrow (or sooner).
- You can even achieve this banner with just a few reviews. My very first book achieved this banner with only 3 reviews. This is 100% true, and the image on the next page is not photoshopped. Also, this was not even my best, final cover, go figure! This is an example of how the #1 New Release banner looks.

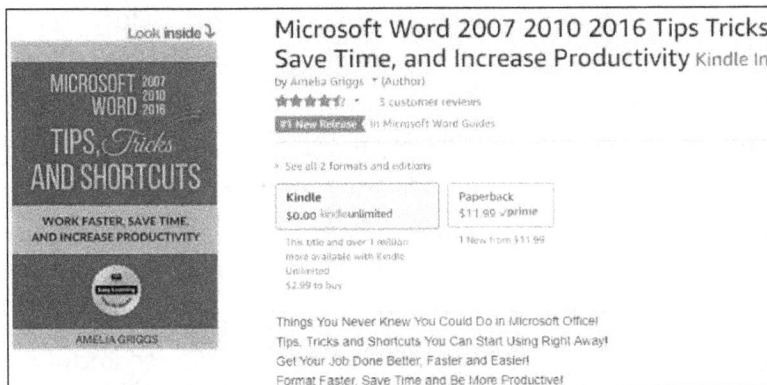

- You will be equally pleased if you see the banner again with your other books (at least I was), but when you see it again, you realize and already know that it doesn't mean as much as you think – but it's still a fantastic feat! Approximately 6 months later, I released an updated version of my first book with a revised cover and title. I used the same strategy and ran a free promo during launch week, and I was able to achieve the #1 New Release banner at that time, with only 6 reviews:

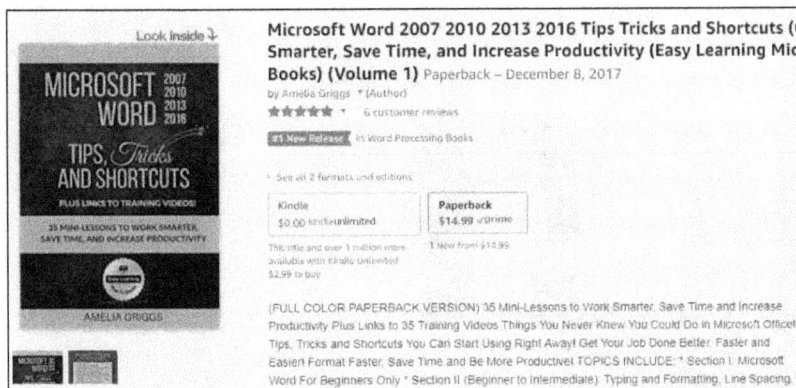

How is it done? If you have a huge following and sell a ton of copies at launch, it can happen naturally. For the rest of us who may not have 1M followers or be a celebrity, it takes a bit of elbow grease.

Here are things you can do to try to achieve the #1 New Release Banner:

- Make sure you have an eBook version of your book.
- Sign up for KDP Select - it's free, and it is for eBooks only.
- Run a free promo at launch for at least 1 day or up to 5 days using KDP Select. For more information on how to use KDP Select, see the section in this book called *KDP, KDP Select and Price Promotions*.
- When you run your free promo, tell as many people as possible that the eBook version of your book is available for free download; the more people that purchase your book for free, the higher the chance that you may achieve the #1 New Release Banner.
- During the free promo period, and on days when your sales are up, check your book listing on Amazon several times a day. Your ranking may change hourly, and this may be the only way to know if you have achieved the #1 New Release Banner. If you see it, take a screen shot to share on social media. You can also frame your screen shot and add it to your wall of book fame!

sAchieving the #1 New Release banner will also give your book increased exposure on Amazon's Hot New Releases page. Customers who search for new releases in your book's categories will see your book listed at the top of the page. All of this helps to promote your book and potentially increase sales!

Amazon Hot New Releases
Our best-selling new and future releases. Updated hourly

‹ Any Department
‹ Books
‹ Computers & Technology
‹ Software
Microsoft
Microsoft Access
Microsoft Excel
Microsoft Office
Microsoft Outlook
Microsoft Powerpoint
Microsoft Project
Microsoft Sharepoint

New Releases in Microsoft Word Guides

1. Microsoft Word 2007...
Amelia Griggs
Paperback

2. kindleunlimited
Microsoft Word 2016 for...
Evgenia Naumchenko
Kindle Edition

#25

The #1 Best Seller Banner

Even more exciting that the #1 New Release banner is the #1 Best Seller banner. You can achieve this as well if your book gets enough activity and sales. This includes sales of free versions of your eBook.

All the dirty little secrets that I listed for the #1 New Release banner are also true about the #1 Best Seller banner. Since Amazon does not tell you when you achieve the #1 Best Seller banner, it is important to check your book listing on Amazon often. Remember to check all formats of your book, including eBook and print versions, since the banner may not always appear on both formats. When you see the banner, scroll down to *Product Details* to look at your rankings. You should also see #1 listed in at least one category, but depending on the sales and other activity, you may see #1 as the ranking in the top three categories listed for your book.

Product details

File Size: 9173 KB
Print Length: 200 pages
Publication Date: June 2, 2018
Sold by: Amazon Digital Services LLC
Language: English
ASIN: B07DH1LF1K
Text-to-Speech: Not enabled
X-Ray: Not Enabled
Word Wise: Not Enabled
Lending: Enabled
Enhanced Typesetting: Not Enabled
Amazon Best Sellers Rank: #2,249 Free in Kindle Store (See Top 100 Free in Kindle Store)
#1 in Kindle Store > Kindle eBooks > Computers & Technology > Networking & Communications > **Networks, Protocols &**
#1 in Kindle Store > Kindle eBooks > Education & Teaching > Teacher Resources > **Computers & Technology**
#1 in Kindle Store > Kindle eBooks > Computers & Technology > Applications & Software > Office Software > **Presentation**

#26

Change your Book Cover

Your book cover is one of the most important aspects of your book. If your book sales and ranking are not what you expected them to be, it's time to revisit the most important features of your book, including the cover. Is your cover genre-appropriate? Remember that readers like to see similar styles when considering books in the same genres. Although you can't change your book's title after publishing, you can change the book cover image. Consider revisiting elements like imagery, font, colors, and style and make sure your cover is the best it can be. This includes the front cover, spine (if applicable) and back cover. Sometimes one little change can make a huge difference in sales and popularity. An example of a small but powerful change is adding a testimonial to the front or back cover. If you do decide to change your book cover, do a new cover reveal and get people excited about your book!

#27

Change Your Book Description

Another important aspect of your book is the description. Your book description should be approximately 150 to 200 words, with a maximum of 4000 characters. Using simple, straightforward, and consumer-friendly terms, the description should tell readers what your book is about and include some key factors to help them decide whether to buy your book.

The first couple sentences are even more important since that is the first thing customers will see when they glance at your book and description. If the first part of your description is not catchy or interesting, potential readers may skip your book altogether. If you book is fiction, include a hook to pique their interest. If your book is nonfiction, what problem does it solve? List the top three reasons why readers may find your book helpful. You can also include a summarized table of contents to tell your audience what is included in your book.

To make your description look nice, you can embed HTML codes in your description as well. Look at descriptions of bestselling books to get an idea of what you might want your description to look like. Begin with a catchy blurb and hook your audience right off the bat. Consider adding some top reviews or testimonials in your book description as well.

Create an Online Presence

#28

Create a Facebook Business Page

When your first book is published, it's perfectly fine to let your family and friends know about your exciting new author venture via Facebook. Family and friends can make great cheerleaders and they will support you and be happy for you; but what you really need is a bigger following and the right audience for your book. Facebook may or may not be the answer, but if you like to use Facebook, consider creating a business page which is separate than your personal Facebook page. To create a business page, just go to www.facebook.com/pages/create or from your personal Facebook page, click on the menu, and select *Create > Page*.

Your Facebook Business Page should include a professional banner image and primarily be dedicated to your book and your business. It may include:

- book announcements
- readings from your book
- book trailers
- pictures of you holding your book
- images or videos of you at author events
- quotes and motivational messages
- helpful information related to your book
- testimonials and reviews

Once you setup your Facebook business page, and after posting a few images and messages, send invites to everyone you know and ask them to *Like* your page. This may include some family and friends, but ideally should include, business associates, entrepreneurs, colleagues, and most importantly – potential readers of your book.

#29

Join Facebook Groups

There are Facebook Groups for just about everything, from cooking, to fitness, to author groups, to small business associations, to parenting groups, to teacher groups, and just about everything else under the sun.

When I first started out, I joined the private Facebook group which was led by the creators of the self-publishing course I invested in. You may have already noticed that this is an ongoing trend. If you sign-up for a free course or a paid course, chances are, there is a corresponding Facebook group. This is a great way to network with the individuals who are also learning and growing while completing the course.

From there, I started joining lots of author groups, some of which were merely support groups, while others were for promoting books. Some groups are more active than others. All groups have rules to follow, and some are stricter than others. Some group admins will remove your post if you are not following the rules for the group. At this point in time, I probably joined over 30 Facebook groups. Initially, I was excited about joining that many groups and envisioned interacting with many of the members and posting about my books, but after a while, it was almost impossible to interact with that many groups. Are joining Facebook groups worth it?

The Pros and Cons of Joining Facebook Groups

Even though I was a member of 30 Facebook groups, overtime I realized that interacting with all the groups I joined was too time consuming. There were only a few groups that I found helpful, and only a handful that truly made a difference. Some groups aren't monitored very closely and then become idle except for other authors posting about their books. Ideally, you want to benefit from groups by posting questions, sharing information, and interacting with other members. In conclusion, even though it is tempting to join dozens of Facebook groups, it's best to just pick a few that help you learn and grow.

#30

Create Your Own Facebook Group

In addition to creating a Facebook business page, you can also consider creating a Facebook Group. Do you need both? The answer is: it depends. Let me elaborate. Both your FB business page and FB group will need your attention. After all, if you build a page or a group, what's the point if you have no visitors or likes, right? If you are planning on having both, there is one way you can have an almost hands-free automatic FB business page – using Instagram.

If you use Instagram, or you are thinking about using Instagram, it's another great way to build up your business. When you post on Instagram, you have the option of also posting the same post on the Facebook page which you have linked to your Instagram account. I use this method and to make sure important posts on my Instagram account also show up on my Facebook business page.

A Facebook page is more about building your brand, while the purpose of a Facebook group is to have more of a discussion platform and a place for members with a similar interest to communicate. With a Facebook group, members can more easily share information and tips with each other.

If you decide to create a Facebook group, the procedure is very similar to creating a Facebook business page.

#31

Create An Amazon Author Page on Author Central

In order to create an author page on Amazon, you will need an Amazon Author Central account. This does require that you have at least one book self-published on KDP. Once you have met Amazon's guidelines, to get started with Author Central, go to *https://authorcentral.amazon.com* and click *Join Now*. You can sign in using your existing Amazon account information.

Once logged in, you can add your book(s) to your author page. You can also add a profile picture, bio, link to your RSS feed, and more. Author Central is a free tool that you can use to let your readers know more about you and your books.

#32

Create an Author Website

An author website can be as simple as creating a free Facebook page or as complex as setting up an elaborate, customized URL with interactive features, such as an online forum, contact us and a chat option.

Your author page or website should:

- Be easy to navigate
- Offer helpful information
- Contain up-to-date information about your books
- Showcase you and your books

It may also include:

- Your branding images or colors
- Search friendly keywords or keyword phrases
- Sign up link
- Freebies to attract and engage readers

If you already have a blog or website, create a separate page as an author page. Update your home page to include information about your upcoming book with a link to your new author page for future details.

For my blog and website, *https://ameliaswritingcorner.com*, I currently use WordPress, where I post author news, self-publishing information and marketing tips. WordPress is a free, Open-Source application. Although you can use WordPress for free, there may be added costs for a custom domain name, hosting, and added features. It also offers a large array of templates and themes, including themes for authors and writers. Visit *www.wordpress.com* to learn more.

#33

Setup Your LinkedIn Profile

If you haven't setup your LinkedIn profile, which is free, you are missing out. LinkedIn is a great way to network with other professionals and showcase your talents. Your LinkedIn profile includes a banner image, a profile photo, employment history, education, skills, and experience. Even if writing and being an author is not related to your field of work, you can still include your books and other publications under the *Accomplishments* section of your profile. Under *Accomplishments*, you can include *Publications, Patents, Courses, Projects, Honors and Awards, Test Scores, Languages* and *Organizations*. Click *Publications* to add your books to this section.

#34

Create Marketing Videos

Consider creating a YouTube channel to announce and talk about your books. The advantage to having a YouTube channel is that you can monitor the analytics and better identify who is interested in your book. Apps like TubeBuddy, which has a free plan and paid plans, offer an array of additional tools and analytics. The most expensive plans offer you the most tools, strategies and statistics. My favorite TubeBuddy tool is the Keyword Planner, which helps you identify popular keyword phrases to use when adding tags to your video. Consider creating not one marketing video, but several. For example:

Self-Help Book Videos - If you wrote a self-help book, this is an easy genre to discuss on a video because you can offer tips, create explainer videos, or offer a help session where you address common questions on your topic and then provide short answers in your video.

Memoir Book Videos - If you wrote a memoir, create a picture gallery of life events, and talk about them. Keep the descriptions short to pique their interest in purchasing your book to learn more. You can also consider interviewing other authors who have written memoirs.

Cookbook Videos – If you wrote a cookbook with recipes, post videos of you cooking using the recipes in your book. Include a call to action at the end of the videos showcasing your book cover so your audience knows how to get all the recipes and cooking instructions.

Novels, Short-Stories and Children's Books – If you wrote a novel or fictional story, talk about how you came up with the idea, describe your characters and read a synopsis from your book. Consider inviting potential readers to a live question and answer session.

Promoting on Social Media

#35

Create a Social Media Strategy

Pick the social media platform where you are most active and have the most followers as your primary place to post, and then pick 2 or 3 other platforms to occasionally post. Don't try to post on every social media website, this is time consuming and can stress you out. Remember that you don't have to post every single day. It's easy to get intimated by all the information that other authors are posting frequently. Consider posting weekly or monthly, depending on how much time you have. Just do what you can. It's better to create a quality post weekly or monthly vs. trying to post more frequently about things that don't support your book.

#36

Use Geo-Targeting Links

THIS MARKETING STRATEGY IS A GAME CHANGER! When sharing links to your Amazon book listing on social media, what do you do to make sure potential customers from other countries access the correct link for their region? For example, what if you are in the U.S. and someone from Canada wants to buy your book. Or, what if you are from Canada and someone from Europe wants to buy your book? The answer is: geo-targeting!

In the past, I started including multiple links in my posts, including a book link for U.S., one for Canada, and other countries. This can be cumbersome and time consuming. In addition, if you don't provide links for other countries, customers from other regions may not be able to find your book, and you can potentially lose sales. I started researching options to include a universal link which goes to a specific region.

Although there are various tools available, the tool I currently use is called Genius Link app (geniuslink.com). I found the Genius Link app easy to use and very affordable. You can try it for free and then its's only $5.00 a month.

Amazon also has a free tool available called Amazon OneLink. However, at the time of writing this book, Amazon OneLink is not available for all countries. It is currently only available in 7 countries, vs. Genius Link which is available in 18 countries. There are also some other limitations with Amazon OneLink and a lot more features available with Genius Link. For a comparison of the tools, check out this link: *https://geniuslink.com/vs-onelink*.

I have converted all my book links to genius links, which begin with a prefix of *geni.us (including the period in the middle)*. For example, for the Amazon.com link for my Author Journey Success book is a lengthy, somewhat ugly URL that looks like this:

https://www.amazon.com/gp/product/B0979T7HS8/ref=dbs_a_def_rwt_bibl_vppi_i0

However, the universal Genius Link is a short and sweet custom URL:

https://geni.us/author-ebook1

You can enter any custom name after the *geni.us* prefix and providing it is available, you can use the new shortened, universal Genius Link for your book listing link for all supported countries. The Genius Link app will tell you how many countries have a perfect match for your book. When you share the universal link on your social media, anyone around the world (in the supported countries) can purchase your book from Amazon, and you only need one link!

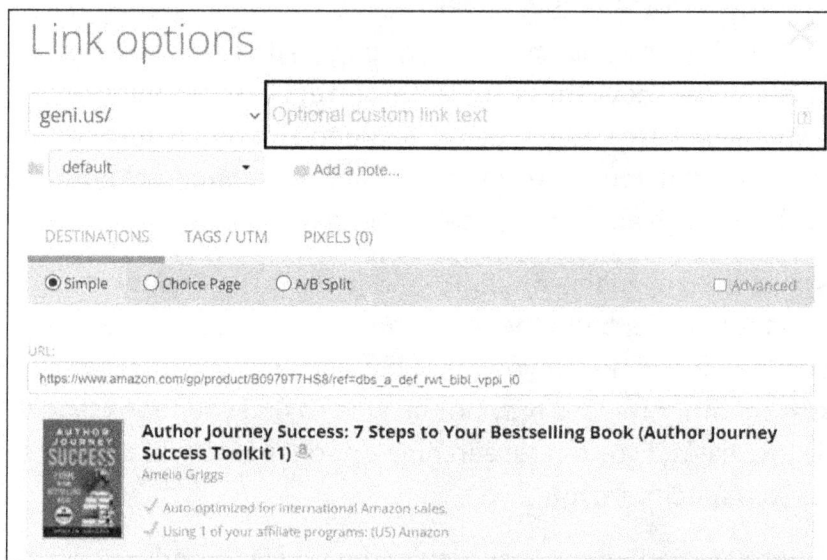

#37

Write Killer Sales Copy

So, you have written a few teaser announcements for your book, and you are excited about the likes and comments you have been receiving; however, how do you turn that into sales? Have you written the best sales copy possible? Does your blurb make customers curious and whet their appetite for more? Doing so can potentially increase customer engagement and may increase the amount of clicks you receive. The more clicks, the higher the chance that those clicks convert into sales.

When you write posts and announcements about your book, create a sense of urgency. Create doubt. Yes, this works. Look at the sentences below. Which one creates a sense of urgency?

- *Do you want to learn how to save money? Learn how in my upcoming book, "How to Save Money"*
- *Are you living paycheck to paycheck? Learn how to save money in 30 days or I will pay your mortgage for 3 months! What are you waiting for? Click here to find out more and get 3 bonus gifts if you buy in the next 15 minutes!*

The first statement above is too general and doesn't include any time restraints or special offers. On the other hand, the second statement creates a sense of urgency and doubt, and it tells the reader that if they don't act now, they might not get free bonus gifts and learn how to have money in a short period of time.

#38

Write an Intriguing Article

Write an interesting article on your blog or website about your book. Relate the article to your book in some way.

If your book solves a problem, write a weekly how-to article. If your book is fiction, consider writing about the character in your book with interactive questions. Get readers interested in reading more details if they purchase your book. Ask readers to follow you to learn more. Add a link to the social media platform of your choice.

If you are more active on social media vs. your blog, create a social media post about the article and then link to the article. Spread the word about your article on multiple social media platforms.

#39

Create a Free Lead Magnet

A lead magnet is a marketing term for a free item or service that you give away for the purpose of gathering contact details. A lead magnet can be a free chapter, a newsletter, a free consultation, or an eBook. You can use lead magnets to create sales leads. One example of a lead magnet is a free sampling of your book. Just make a copy of your manuscript and delete everything except the first few chapters or sections of your book. Make it easy for readers to buy your book. Include a link to your book page, state the benefits of your book and explain why someone should buy your book. Save the document as a PDF, and then use an email service to create a landing page for your free PDF download. If you need a place to upload your free PDF, providing you use Gmail, you can upload your free PDF on Google Drive, and turn on Link Sharing. Right click on the file and select *Share*; in the Get Link section, make sure *Anyone with the link* is selected vs. *Restricted*. Select *Copy Link* and then click *Done*. Ideally, you only want to share the Google Drive link on a sign-up form with an email opt in so you can build email list.

#40

Create a Media Kit

Create a media page including your bio, headshot, book information, links to where people can purchase your book and any related materials. Share your media kit online by adding it to your website, bio, and author page. Media kits may also include your book's ISBN, book title, series title, book description, genre, age category, reader reviews, book formats, pricing, page count, publication date, and links to author interviews. Tools like Canva offer an array of templates for creating a media kit. From the Canva search bar, just search for *Media Kit* to browse through templates. Most are two pages which you can easily customize with your branding colors and information; then download the file as a PDF to post on your website or print copies for in-person events.

#41

Create an Official Book Trailer

This is different than creating marketing videos. Your book trailer should be a professional video about your book including animation and either music or voiceover. There are a multitude of apps you can use to create a book trailer for free. However, if time is of the essence and you don't have experience creating promotional videos, you can hire someone on Fiverr to create a beautiful book trailer for you for a nominable cost.

Once your book trailer is created, post it everywhere on social media, including a link on where readers can purchase your book.

#42

Use TikTok to Promote Your Book

TikTok is not just for posting dancing videos or cat videos. It can also be used as a promotional tool for products including books. To promote books, just include the hashtag #booktok in the description for your post. Posts can be up to 150 characters. This may potentially increase the views and watch time for your post. Consider talking about your book and show the cover as well as a few pages on the inside. It's easy to create a short video on your mobile phone on TikTok. Just use the plus sign in the app to get started; select the *Camera* option to record live or use the *Upload* option to upload a video that you previously recorded. Remember to record the video using portrait orientation vs. landscape. Consider recording a video outdoors where lighting is better than indoors.

Note: Popular hashtags, as well as the video time limits can change over time. At the time of writing this book, #booktok is most popular hashtag for promoting books.

#43

Use Instagram and Tags

On Instagram, post book promo graphics, teasers from your book, book quotes, paragraphs from your book, and your book cover. Don't just tell people to buy your book; instead, offer them helpful information in the form of a tip, advice, or freebie. Be sure to include relevant hashtags which can potentially boost engagement and discoverability of your post. You can include up to 30 hashtags in your description, which you can add at the bottom of your post, or in a separate comment in your post. Some popular hashtags include #bookstagram, #booklover, #booknerd, #bookstack, and #instabook.

#44

Promote on Pinterest

Pinterest is yet another great platform to post and share images and videos related to your book. It's easy, free, and fun to create pins on Pinterest and you can organize your pins on boards for different types of categories. To promote your books on Pinterest:

- Create an author board.
- Pin pictures of bock mockups.
- Pin pictures of readers with your book.
- Create pins with links to a free sampling of your book.
- Interact with similar pins and boards to build a following.

#45

Tweet on Twitter

Twitter is yet another social media platform where you can share short posts of no more than 280 characters called tweets with your followers. Tweet about book reviews, book news, book events, and any new information you want to share about your book. If you don't have a following on Twitter, you can start by following others and interacting with other authors, book enthusiasts and business owners. Twitter users can like, comment on, or retweet your posts to their followers.

#46

Promote on LinkedIn

In addition to setting up your LinkedIn profile, which was covered earlier in this book, you can create a post on LinkedIn. You can insert a promotional photo or video, add a post about an event, or choose the *Write Article* option to publish an article on LinkedIn as part of your feed. The content for your posts doesn't have to be brand new content; you can leverage existing content from your other posts on other social media platforms. There's also a section called *Featured* where you can select posts, articles, links, or media to be featured at the top of your LinkedIn page.

#47

Interview Someone

Contact other authors or business owners you know to ask if they want to be interviewed. If your focus is on business, consider interviewing an entrepreneur. If you wrote a children's book, interview a successful children's book author. If you wrote a cookbook, interview a chef at a popular restaurant. Invite people you know, but also ask the person being interviewed to invite individuals in their business circle as well. This will increase the audience and promote both you and the person getting interviewed. The interview can be a series of questions and answers in an article posted on your blog or website, or it can a video recording posted on your YouTube channel or other platform.

#48

Get Interviewed on a Podcast

Ask podcasters to consider interviewing you on their podcast show or channel. Talking about your book on other people's podcasts, YouTube channel and platforms will:

- Build authority and trust
- Helps you build your network with others successful business owners
- Increases your audience
- Can help to build social proof

Online Ads

#49

Amazon Ads

When I first tried to setup Amazon ads, I quickly realized that there are specific strategies to learn to make the most of these types of ads. It's important to educate yourself on how to setup Amazon ads by investing some time and research. There are a multitude of videos on the topic on YouTube. Amazon also has a plethora of resources including an online blog with online advertising best practices, certification training, tips, guided learning, and an FAQ list. Some of the resources can be overwhelming. I found Bryan's Cohen Amazon Ad Challenge very helpful. At the time of writing this book, he offers the challenge several times a year. The challenge is free and requires some commitment for a few weeks as there is homework to complete. If you need more extensive help, he offers a course as well.

Overall, for Amazon ads to be successful, it's important to target your audience correctly. In addition, it's pertinent that you monitor your statistics and insights to determine what worked and didn't work so that you can adjust your ads accordingly for optimum results. As far as the cost of Amazon ads, this depends on your bid amount and other factors when setting up your ad.

To access Amazon Ads from the KDP dashboard, click *Marketing* from the menu across the top; then look for the section entitled *Amazon Ads*, where you can choose a marketplace and create a campaign, register for an Amazon Ads webinar, or enroll in free Amazon Ads training courses.

You can also access Amazon Ads by visiting *https://advertising.amazon.com* and signing in with your existing KDP/Amazon login.

You can learn more about Amazon Ads for books by visiting: *https://advertising.amazon.com/solutions/industries/book-ads*

Finally, remember that there is no magic formula when it comes to Amazon ads. Monitor your campaign statistics frequently, especially when running your ads for the first time. It takes time and practice, but it can make a positive difference in your book sales and activity.

#50

Facebook Ads

To advertise on Facebook, you have the option of using *Boost Post* or creating a Facebook ad in Ads Manager. After posting on a business Facebook page, you will see a *Boost Post* option on the bottom of the post. The *Boost Post* option is considered an ad and will require you select your target audience, your budget, and the length of time to run the ad. Facebook ads are created through Ads Manager and offer more advanced customization solution such as ad placement options, ad objectives, and advanced targeting capabilities. Costs will vary depending on what you select for your budget amount.

Facebook Ads are fairly simple to setup by using the *Boost Post* option on business page posts. I didn't research or study Facebook ads to set them up. However, if you want to learn more about Facebook Ads and the Ads Manager, you can visit the link below, which is helpful in providing statistics including how much you spent on ads and the status of ads.

https://www.facebook.com/business/tools/ads-manager.

#51

Instagram Ads

Instagram and Facebook operate on the same ad platform, so running ads on either platform is done in a similar fashion. *Note*: Facebook bought Instagram on April 9, 2012, for $1 billion. Depending on how active you are on either platform, you can try running ads on either Instagram or Facebook, or both. You can use the *View Insights* option to see how your ad performed and decide if you want to run the ad again. Costs will vary depending on what you select for your budget amount.

#52

Pinterest Ads

If you are active on Pinterest, running ads on Pinterest will give your pins extra exposure in relevant search results. To get started, select the *Promote* option for an existing pin; then select your options including targeting, audience size, ad duration and budget. If you have a Pinterest Business account, you can promote your best-performing pins, create a video, or promote an image that's been pinned from a website. Costs will vary depending on what you select for your budget amount.

#53

TikTok Ads

To run ads on TikTok, there are certain requirements needed to quality. The TikTok advertising platform is separate than a TikTok account and profile. First, you would need to create a TikTok advertising account. In addition, you may need to submit information to see if your business qualities. Once your advertising account is setup and approved, from the TikTok Ads dashboard, click the *Campaign* tab at the top of the page; then click *Create*. Then select campaign options such as a campaign objective or the primary target for your campaign. Costs will vary depending on what you select for your budget amount.

#54

LinkedIn Ads

With LinkedIn ads, you can generate leads, drive website traffic, and build brand awareness. Since LinkedIn focuses on your career and business, it's important to promote your books as part of your business. You can leverage posts from other social media platforms and share them on LinkedIn.

Costs will vary depending on the type of activity you are paying for and the ad auction.

Book Promotion Services

This section covers various book promotion sites. There are hundreds and possibly thousands of book promotion services online. Some are worth a try to see what works best for you. Choosing which book promotion service is best depends on your needs and budget. Some are free but may require you to opt in with your email address. For the ones which are not free, the cost varies per website. Some sites have specific submission guidelines and may or may not accept your book. In addition, some promotion websites are only for eBooks.

Note: Be wary of book promotion sites which claim to guarantee book sales or make other promises. There are no guarantees that any book promotion websites will make you any sales, but what it will do is increase exposure for your book. If you are not sure about the validity and safety of a book promotion website, you can use *https://safeweb.norton.com* to check a website. It's also very important to do your research and look for reviews and testimonials for book promotion services and websites as well.

#55

BargainBooksy

In order to advertise on BargainBooksy, your book must be between .99 and $5.00, and over 50 pages, so this option may not work well with most children's books or short books. BargainBooksy has over 317,000 registered users, so a BargainBooksy feature can help you to drive sales of your book, find a new audience of readers, generate reviews for your book, and improve your book rank on retail sites. Pricing ranges from $20 to $220 based on the genre of your book. For more info, visit: *https://www.bargainbooksy.com/sell-more-books*

Note: If you are planning this for a book launch, be sure to book it in advance. You may find that it is sold out and you might have to wait for an open date. They also limit author promotion to one feature per book per 30 days.

#56

BookBub

BookBub.com offers fee-based ads and promotions which can be quite expensive but they also offer free marketing tools as well via this link: _https://www.bookbub.com/partners/free_tools_.

Using their free tools, you can:

- Create a free author profile including your bio, an image and a list of your books. You can share your author bio, and also network with other BookBub subscribers and build a following.
- Download the free eBook, _The Ultimate Collection of Book Marketing Examples_ which includes author websites (including screen shots of their home pages), author bio examples, Facebook cover designs, Instagram profiles and Pinterest profiles as well.
- Use _BookBub Recommendations_ which is a free way for authors to engage with readers; authors can post recommendations by clicking "Review" on any book's page on BookBub.com. Once an author posts a recommendation, it will appear in their followers' recommendations feed on BookBub.com. Followers will receive alerts about recommendations via a weekly digest email. In order to benefit, you will need to have a following on BookBub.
- Download _The Ultimate Guide to Book Marketing_ which is a series of links to many of their posts about marketing.
- Setup New Release Alerts – Just like Amazon alerts follows of your Amazon Author of your new releasees, BookBub can also do the same. When you come out with a new release, BookBub will alert your followers. Again, you would have to have BookBub followers for this option to be beneficial.

#57

BookFunnel

BookFunnel.com offers a variety of author services, including delivery of your eBook as a reader magnet, author swaps and group promos, customized landing pages, and email integration. BookFunnel is not free and offers several types of plans starting at $20/month. To view all their plans, visit: https://bookfunnel.com/pricing

#58

BookSends

To advertise on booksend.com, your book needs to have at least 5 reviews, with a high overall average, and an attractive cover. In addition, you need to have a planned sale price of less than $3 and at least 50% off full price. They will not feature the same book more than once every 90 days. Their ad prices range from $10 to $120 depending on genre and the price of your eBook. https://booksends.com/advertise.php

#59

BookRaid

BookRaid.com advertises via their newsletter which is sent to over 30,000 active email subscribers. They charge a fee per click so the costs depend on your CTR (Click Through Rate). However, all promotions have a maximum spend of $60.

#60

BuckBooks

Buckbooks.net has two different types of promotions available. The higher-end promotion is quite expensive. You can sign up to be promoted in their daily deals broadcast along with 5 to 7 other authors for $29.00; or, for $100, you can sign up for a featured solo broadcast, which they do once a week. They feature your book, series, or a lead magnet to the Buck Books subscribers. To promote on buckbooks.net, you need to complete a book promotion application for promotion approval. For more info, visit: *https://buckbooks.net/promotions*.

#61

ENT (Ereader News Today)

Ereader News Today offers promotions for both free eBooks and books priced at up to $2.99. They promote on their website (*ereadernewstoday.com*), their social media sites, (Facebook, Twitter, Pinterest, etc.) and in their daily newsletter. Promotions are scheduled up to 30 days ahead of time. Before submitting your book, read their list requirements and other factors to consider for approval. Pricing ranges from $45 to $120 depending on the genre of your book. For more info, visit:

https://www.ereadernewstoday.com/bargain-and-free-book-submissions.

#62

Free Booksy

Your book must be free to qualify for a feature on Freebooksy (*www.freebooksy.com/for-the-authors*). They have over 547,000 registered readers and they include a homepage feature, inclusion in their daily email and a post to over 200K+ Facebook fans. Prices range from $30 to $230, depending on the genre. If you have a perma-free book, or a free eBook promotion coming up through KDP Select, it might be something to consider for promoting a book series. See pricing and other information here: *https://www.freebooksy.com/freebooksy-feature-pricing-4*

#63

Prolific Works (formerly InstaFreebie)

Prolific works (*www.prolificworks.com*), formerly InstaFreebie, is a site where you can give your eBook away in exchange for the reader's email address. The service is not free, and packages start at $20/month. So why would you want to pay a fee to give your book away? In this case, it's all about building connections with readers who are interested in your book. This type of promotion works best if you have more than one book. With other book promotion sites, you are paying for your book to be advertised, but there's no guarantee that it will results in sales. With Prolific Works, even though you are giving about your eBook for free, you are getting the readers' email addresses. You can then contact these readers when the next book in your series is available. They have three pricing options as follows: a basic free plan, a Plus package of $20 a month, or a Pro package of $50 a month. To learn more about their packages visit: *https://www.prolificworks.com/plans*.

#64

The Fussy Librarian

The Fussy Librarian advertises your book by including it in a daily email. It will be included in their searchable database for 30 days as part of your fee. At the time of writing, they have over 460,000 email subscribers. The number of subscribers per genre varies. Go to the *Advertising* tab on their website to check for available dates per genre. *http://www.thefussylibrarian.com*. Prices ranges from $11 to $21 depending on the genre.

Goodreads Author Opportunities

Goodreads is the world's largest site for readers and book recommendations with a mission of helping people find and share books they love. It is a subsidiary of Amazon that allows readers to search its database of books, annotations, quotes, and reviews. This section highlights various tools and opportunities on Goodreads for promoting books, all of which are free.

#65

Goodreads Author Program

The Goodreads Author Program is a free tool for authors which allow you to create an author page, promote your books, and interact with readers. Once your author profile is completed and approved, it will include the official Goodreads Author badge, which you can use to tell your fans to follow you on Goodreads. Be sure to add a profile picture, update your bio, and confirm all your books which will be shown on your author page. To get started, visit: *http://www.goodreads.com/author/program*

#66

Goodreads Author Blogs

Although there are millions of Goodreads members, Goodreads Authors are the only Goodreads members who can have a blog on the site. When you write a new blog post, it will be published to your Goodreads Author blog and to your friends' and followers' updates feeds, depending on their individual settings. If you already have an author blog, you can sync your external blog directly to your author profile on Goodreads via your Author Dashboard. Just click *View Your Blog,* select the option to sync with a pre-existing blog, enter your blog's URL and click Save. This will give you and your blog increased exposure for promoting your books.

#67

Link Your Goodreads and Kindle Accounts

If you have a Goodreads account as well as a Kindle account, you can link the accounts together to synchronize information across both platforms. Although there are general advantages, such as automatically updating your reading progress, seeing updates and recommendations from your kindle device, and instant access to new books, the biggest advantage for authors is that reviews for your books will automatically be posted on both Amazon and Goodreads.

#68

Goodreads Ask the Author

Shortly after you join Goodreads and setup your author profile, turn on the *Ask the Author* feature on your dashboard. This is a Q&A platform that allows readers to submit questions to Goodreads Authors anytime, directly from an author's profile. *Ask the Author* is unique because it doesn't make questions visible to the public until the author chooses to answer them, giving the author control over when and how to respond. Answering reader questions allows you to connect and interact with readers and authors all over the world. These readers might share their conversation with their friends and followers on Goodreads, thereby giving you and your book increased exposure.

#69

Review Books on Goodreads

Consider reviewing or adding at least 25 books to your *want-to-read* shelf on Goodreads. This will help readers learn what books their favorite authors have enjoyed. Remember to post reviews for books you have read as well. Posting reviews keeps your name in front of readers who follow you and enhances your Goodreads profile.

#70

Join a Goodreads Group

Just like Facebook groups, LinkedIn groups, etc., Goodreads groups is another opportunity to connect and engage with readers and authors. Comment and Like posts in groups. Post helpful information, answer questions and support other authors. To view Goodreads groups, visit: *https://www.goodreads.com/group.*

#71

Run a Goodreads Giveaway

Running a giveaway on Goodreads can create buzz around your book and potentially earn you some reviews. You can run a giveaway for a print book or a Kindle book. I opted to run a Goodreads giveaway from 8/22/21 through 8/30/21 for two main reasons: there was a huge 50% off Goodreads Giveaway sale during the month of August 2021, and I needed a way to promote the first book in my Author Journey Success series. My goal was to get readers interested in my book series. I monitored my stats daily and watched the entries climb, and that part was exciting to see.

I took screenshots periodically to keep track of the progress. At the end of my giveaway, I was very happy with my stats. There were 907 entrants, 862 shelved as *Want to Read*, and 100 winners. Goodreads automatically delivered the eBook version to the winners. In addition, because I purchased the Premium giveaway, Goodreads also sends a follow-up reminder email to the winners a few weeks later to encourage them to post a review.

Note: This strategy can be quite expensive. A standard giveaway is $119, and a premium giveaway is $599. The least expensive option is the standard giveaway using your eBooks. Whether you give away 10 eBooks or 100 eBooks, the price of the giveaway is a flat fee. However, if you opt to give away a print book, you pay for the cost of your print books and you are required to ship the books. In my case, the eBook version made the most sense.

#72

Write a Quote on Goodreads

The Quotes feature in the Community tab in Goodreads allows readers and authors to search for quotes by keyword or author name. There are quotes by famous writers, celebrities and authors from around the world! As a Goodreads Author, you can post a quote as well. When you add a quote, Goodreads members can see your quotes. The more Likes you get, the more popular your quotes will become. Categories for Quotes include *Popular*, *Recent*, *New*, *Friends* and *New Authors*.

Adding a quote is easy, fun and can potentially increase your engagement and exposure on Goodreads. If someone likes a unique quote that you post, they may visit your profile and take a look at your books as well. To view quotes or add your own quote, visit: *https://www.goodreads.com/quotes*.

Creative Ways to Promote Your Book

#73

Re-Release Your Book

Once your book is live and your marketing strategies are underway, what if you have done everything you can possibly do but your sales are just mediocre? Now is the time to set new goals and go a step further – you must now go back and re-read your book in detail and decide how you can make it better. There's always room for improvements. Are you sure you proofed the interior enough times? Can you add any free gifts, perks, or any other content to make your book stand out from the crowd?

This can work with any type of book! I like to write in different genres, and I can tell you for sure this will give your book a big boost no matter what the genre.

On June 29, 2017, I released my first book with a so-so cover design and amateur marketing strategies.

On December 8, 2017, just six months later, I re-released my first book with a new improved cover design, additional formats (including an eBook, black and white paperback, and color paperback), and improvements to the interior, including optimized screen shots, and links to companion videos. This was truly a lesson learned as it was my first book. As I continued to move forward with the second and third book in my technology series, I continued to experiment with formats, trim sizes, and more marketing strategies. Here's a low-down of what I did to improve the books in my first series, which was a technology book series:

Book 1: Microsoft Word Tips, Tricks and Shortcuts

- **Cover Design Update** – I updated the cover design with improved contrasting colors of yellow and dark blue. I also incorporated additional text on the back and front cover to showcase the book. Finally, I created a branding emblem to be used throughout all my books and added it to the book cover.
- **Book Description Update** – I optimized my book description by adding HTML to add bold and other formatting to enhance the text and layout.

- **Book Category Update** – I revisited my book categories and contacted KDP for any category change requests.

Book 2: Microsoft Excel Tips, Tricks and Shortcuts

- **Series Cover Design with a Color Twist -** Leveraging the improved cover design for book 1, I utilized the same design but used a green textured background since people associate Excel with a green color.
- **B&W vs. Color Paperback Experiment -** I asked myself, *"What do the people want"*? To help me decide which paperback format I wanted to offer with regards to B&W vs. color interior, I posted some surveys on Facebook. I was originally only going to offer B&W interior to keep the cost down. However, the consensus after the survey was that people seemed to want the color paperback vs. black and white for this type of book, which includes lots of screenshots. As an experiment, I decided to offer a color paperback version for my Excel book. The downside to this is that color paperbacks are a lot more expensive to print so the retail cost must be higher to earn the same profit as you would for B&W interior.

Book 3: Microsoft PowerPoint Tips, Tricks and Shortcuts

- **Series Cover Design with Another Color Twist -** Leveraging the improved cover design for books 1 and 2 in this series, I utilized the same design but used a reddish/burgundy textured background since people associate PowerPoint with this color.
- **Large Print B&W Paperback Experiment -** As far as formats, I still offered eBook format for my third book but for paperback format, I decided to try something new. In addition to offering a color paperback, since I needed more room to show additional graphics and screen prints, I started going through my bookshelves at home and in libraries, in search of textbooks to once again look for new ideas. The 7" X 10" trim size I had been using all along served my books well for the most part, and I liked that size better than the smaller 6" X 9" trim size. However, I wanted to go bigger for the PowerPoint book. In addition, I felt like the overall text size could be bigger too. I started researching the possibility of using something called Large Print and decided that was the best option. I decided to expand the trim size to 8" X 10", which allowed me to show wider graphics. In addition, I change the font size

to 16 pt. and checked the box for Large Print when uploading this version of my book. Large Print is listed under the *Format* options for Amazon book categories. Now, years later, the Large Print B&W edition of my PowerPoint Tips, Tricks and Shortcut book continues to be one of my biggest sellers.

Here is an example of one of the announcements I posted all over social media for the re-release of one of one of my books:

> **BOOK RE-RELEASE NEWS:** *The 2nd edition of my book, Microsoft Word Tips, Tricks and Shortcuts, which contains 35 mini-lessons on Microsoft Word now contains links to 35 companion videos! I have redesigned the cover, title and subtitle and made enhancements throughout! The eBook version is available on Amazon, and the Paperback version is coming soon. I've contacted Amazon to request that the 2nd edition be pushed out to everyone who has purchased the eBook. Amazon has confirmed that the number of changes are significant enough to push it out to previous purchases. If you already purchased this eBook, please be sure to update your Kindle library to ensure that the latest version is downloaded. If you have any issues, please feel free to contact me.*

What happens to my old version if I release a new version?

If you upload a new interior and/or a new book cover (with the same title), using the book listing, the new version will replace the old version. This is free on KDP and you can update the interior or exterior as many times as needed. The original publication date remains the same. If you want your audience to know that your book has been updated, consider adding a note in the Amazon book description. This can be done by editing book details in KDP bookshelf.

If you decide to change the title and/or have a completely new version of the interior, and opt to create a brand-new book listing, then the old version of your book will remain on Amazon. You can unpublish your book if you no longer want to offer it for sale, but it will remain on Amazon with an *unavailable* status. Instead, what you can do is a note at the beginning of the description for the old edition that says: *New Version Now Available*. Include a link and information on how they can find the new version.

What about people who already bought my book? Will they get a new version?

If you make a lot of changes to the interior, you can contact KDP and ask them to consider pushing your revised version out to anyone who has already purchased an eBook version of your book. They will evaluate the revisions and determine if the changes are significant enough to provide a new version to previous purchasers.

An enhanced front cover probably won't be enough for KDP to push your book out to your reader's Kindle library, but you can consider creating a few promotional graphics to share everywhere on social media to alert your followers about your revised cover.

#74

Create a QR Code for Your Book or Website

For print books, such as paperback and hardcover, having a QR code which links to your book, author website or social media makes perfect sense. This is a free and easy way to help customers reach you and your website in a snap! You can create one or more QR codes to link to different social media platforms, your blog, book review pages and anywhere you want your audience to visit. For my technology series, I created companion videos for each chapter in my books. At the end of each chapter, I included a QR code which readers could scan to quickly visit my YouTube channel.

Note: Previously, there was a Scan Code option in the Wallet app on iPhones, but now you can scan a QR code using your camera app if using an iPhone. Most mobile devices can scan a QR code either automatically or through a QR scanner app.

🖥 **Watch the Demo**

Click here to see a demo on how to create a QR code for free using the Unitag App. You can also use the following link:
https://www.youtube.com/hashtag/ezqrcodes

#75

Put Your Product in Front of People

You can use this strategy in person and online. At in-person events, such as book festivals, stand – don't sit, and greet any visitors with a smile. Next, strike up a conversation by greeting them warming and ask them if they have any questions or want to take a closer look at your book. You can also present them with a flyer or media kit page. Consider handing them your book so they can take a look. Once in their hand, they will be more inclined to look inside, and they may potentially purchase your book as well.

For online events, although you can't get your physical book in front of them like an in-person event, you can offer them a peek inside. You can show some of the inside of your book by posting images of several pages, creating a video flipping through some of the pages, or by going live and sharing your screen with your eBook open. Consider discussing some of the content to pique their interest. Remember to include a link to tell them how to purchase your book.

Whether in-person or online, the goal is to get people to look and see your product.

#76

Learn Canva

Throughout this book, I have mentioned how you can use Canva for promotional graphics and lots of other content. Since Canva has been so helpful and versatile for my own marketing, I wanted to help other authors learn about all the features too. Learning Canva can help you create your own promotional graphics vs. hiring someone to create them for you. I created a 1-hour Canva overview tutorial which is totally free and available on my YouTube channel. I'm also working on a Canva course as well.

Here's what's included in my Canva overview tutorial:

- 00:00 - 00:46 Introduction | What's Included
- 00:46 - 02:16 Canva Dashboard
- 02:17 - 08:37 Canva Templates Overview

- 08:38 - 18:29 Create a Graphic Using a Template
- 18:30 - 24:28 Editing, Changing Colors, Adding Elements
- 24:29 - 29:30 Customizing a Branding Template Graphic
- 29:31 - 38:07 Creating Graphics from Scratch
- 38:08 - 57:14 Canva Tips, Tricks and Secrets! (Includes Inserting Music and Videos)
- 57:15 - 59:08 A Few More Ways to Find Things in Canva

You can search for the tutorial on YouTube using the hashtag *#ezcanva* or just go to: *https://www.youtube.com/hashtag/ezcanva*.

To learn more about my online courses, please visit:

https://ameliaswritingcorner.com/courses

To try Canva Pro for free, visit: *geni.us/getcanva*

KDP Marketing Resources

In addition to KDP Select and Author Central, KDP offers various other marketing resources, all of which are available on the *Marketing* section of the KDP dashboard. To use these resources, you would need a login to KDP, and at least one book published on KDP. Some features only apply to eBooks.

#77

Add A+ Content

The *A+ Content* feature on KDP allows you to add images, text, and comparison tables to your product detail page to engage readers and provide more information about your book. From the KDP dashboard, select *Marketing* from the menu across the top. To learn more about *A+ Content*, select *Getting Started with A+ Content*, *A+ Content Guidelines*, or *A+ Content Examples*. Once you are ready to add A+ Content, choose your marketplace, and then select Manage *A+ Content*.

#78

Nominate your eBook

Providing you have an eBook published on KDP, you can nominate your eBook to be included in Kindle Deals and Prime Reading promotional programs to reach new readers. Although nominations do not guarantee enrollment, you can nominate up to two eBooks at a time for Kindle Deals and one eligible eBook at a time for Prime Reading. If your eBook is selected, KDP sends you an email with the details and you can accept or decline the offer.

Kindle Deals are limited-time discount deals offered on eBooks, lasting from one day or up to multiple weeks. Customers will see both the regular price and the promotional price on the eBook's detail page. In addition, eBooks enrolled in Kindle Deals may be eligible to be featured in the Kindle store. To be eligible for Kindle Deals your eBook must be enrolled in the 70% royalty plan (US marketplace only). To be eligible for Prime Reading, your eBooks must be enrolled in KDP Select.

Prime Reading is an optional promotional program that helps authors get their titles in front of Amazon's most engaged readers. Prime Reading members enjoy unlimited reading at no additional cost.

To nominate your eBook(s), from the KDP dashboard, select *Marketing*. Under *Nominate Your eBooks*, click *Nominate a book* and follow the instructions for the nomination process. By default, nominations are automatically renewed at the end of 90 days. To turn this feature off, uncheck the auto-renew checkbox.

#79

Gifting for Kindle

This feature allows you to gift your eBooks to readers at an event or send copies to newsletter subscribers. You can promote your book by purchasing a copy to send to specific people, or you can purchase multiple copies to offer to a larger audience.

Here's how it works:

- If you want to gift your eBook to one person, Amazon sends the recipient a redemption code; the recipient can choose to accept your eBook gift by redeeming the code.
- You can also purchase multiple copies of your eBook in a single order. In that case, instead of reception codes, a set of redemption links are sent to the recipients. Recipients cannot exchange eBooks for gift cards or other products.

To learn more about Gifting for Kindle, from the *Marketing* page on your KDP dashboard, see the *More Marketing Resources* section.

#80

Kindle Instant Book Previews

Kindle instant previews allow you to share a preview of your eBook as a link via email, text, and other favorite apps. By sharing a free book preview or embedding it on a website, anyone can read a sample of your book without signing in to Amazon.

From your desktop browser, search for the eBook version of your book. Click the *Embed* link next to the other sharing options.

Copy the URL or embed the HTML code to share. You can share the URL anywhere on social media or send it to readers directly to share an instant preview of your book.

To learn more about Kindle Instant Book Previews, from the *Marketing* page on your KDP dashboard, see the *More Marketing Resources* section.

"Go the Extra Mile" Ways to Promote Your Book

#81

Use a CTA

Put a Call to Action (CTA) at the end of your book. Readers who reach the end of your book most likely want to say involved with you and your book. Remember to include links at the back of your book on how to post a review, how to sign up for your newsletter and how readers can find you on social media. Include a thank you page along with the call to action to show your appreciation to your readers for reading your book.

#82

Reach Out to Radio Stations

This may take a bit of elbow grease but may potentially get you a spot or shout out on live radio. Consider contacting local radio stations, let them know you are a local author, and ask them if you can be featured on a radio ad or talk show. Remember to have information about you and your book on-hand to share. Opportunities and fees may vary depending on the radio station. It doesn't hurt to ask. You can search on Fiverr and look for gigs on promoting your book on radio.

#83

Contact Newspapers, Magazines and Ezines

Reach out to local, newspapers, journals, and magazines. Some newspapers require that you purchase ads to be featured, while others may provide opportunities to be featured for free. I had experiences with both fee-based and free features.

Here is my experience with a fee-based feature article opportunity:

My Feature Article: There is a local newspaper in my area published by a company named Times Publishing Newspaper. Over the years, I noticed several local authors were featured in their newspaper. I contacted them to inquire, and they did have a requirement that I purchased 3 months of ads (1 ad per month) for a feature story. I decided to embark on the investment, and I was thrilled with outcome. The editor wrote an article based on a phone interview and included a photo of me and my books as well.

To view the electronic version of the completed article, visit: _geni.us/amelia1_

Here is my experience with a *free* feature article opportunity:

My Feature Article: After all of my 3 children's rhyming books were live, I was searching online to see if my books came up on Google searches, and I accidentally found a magazine called *Bella Magazine*. I found the magazine was a perfect fit for my books because the main character is named *Bella*. In addition, the magazine was geared for women and business. I reached out to the publisher and owner of the magazine, which was called Beck Media Group and explained my background, why and how I wrote my children's books, and how I was striving to be an entrepreneur. She not only agreed to feature me in an article, but there was no charge for the article. She featured me in the February 2020 issue of her magazine! In addition, she sent me a few copies of the printed magazine. I was beyond thrilled.

To view the electronic version of the completed article, visit: _geni.us/amelia2_

#84

Do a Joint Promotion

Team up with other authors to do a joint promotion. This can be an online promotion or held during an author event. Although joint promotions can be done across different genres, it may work better if you work with authors in the same or similar genre.

You may have seen posts on social media or even via email newsletters where multiple books are shown. In this case, one author takes the lead to collect images of other author's books and creates a post with all the book images. A short synopsis of each book may also be included. If three different authors with 3 different email lists share the same joint promotion post, this increases the exposure for all authors' books. The same is true if a promotional post is shared on social media for multiple authors. The more followers everyone has, the higher the exposure and promotional opportunity for everyone's books.

The cost of joint promotions varies from free to fee-based depending on the type of promotion. First, try collaborating for free with several other authors as a starting point. There are also joint promotion opportunities you can look for on websites such as Fiverr.com. Start with a small budget to test the waters to see if it's a good fit for your book and be sure to read reviews before you purchase any promotions.

#85

Consolidate Your Links

Once you start creating an author site, business page, Instagram profile, and other social media pages, it becomes increasingly difficult to know which link you should share. In addition, you need an easy way to keep track of all your links. You can consolidate all your links using an app called Link Tree (*linktr.ee/login*) They have a free option as well as a Pro option which is currently $6/month. Here is an example of my Link Tree: *linktr.ee/ameliagriggs*

#86

Update Your Email Signature

Setup your email signature, including your name, contact info, book title and book information. Most email programs allow you to customize your email signature, which is a great way to share information about you and your books. Earlier in this book, I mentioned how to use Genius Link for geo-targeting, which is #36 in this book.

In your email signature, consider including a geo-targeted link for you book(s), your main author website, and your Link Tree link for all your other links.

#87

Sign-up for Amazon Affiliate Programs

To earn even more royalty for your books, apply for the Amazon Associates program, which helps content creators, publishers and bloggers monetize their traffic. There is no charge to apply, and there is no minimum referral requirement or quota you must reach before earning referral fees with their program. To learn more, visit:

https://affiliate-program.amazon.com/welcome/getstarted

Once you sign-up and get approved, you will be assigned a unique ID for tracking activity and sales. This can be used for selling your books or any other related products.

#88

Re-Purpose Your Content

Do you have content on-hand that you can share to help others? If you write nonfiction, this can be a problem that you have solved. If you write fiction, how did you come up with your character names? How did you start writing? Repurpose your content by creating courses, YouTube videos, workbooks, and content marketing. Offer tips, tricks, and information to help people and use different methods to share the content.

#89

Offer Multiple Formats

Did you create multiple formats for your book? Ideally, you want to have at least an eBook version and a print version. Other formats include hardcover and audio books. In some cases, this may not apply. For example, for a workbook, you might only offer a printed version.

If you opted for multiple formats including paperback and eBook, are your books linked together? KDP automatically links formats of the same book together. This is especially helpful for potential buyers so they can see all formats available for purchasing your book. If for some reason, different formats of your book are not linked together, you can contact them to inquire. There is one exception: If you have both B&W as well as color paperback, KDP will only link one of your paperbacks with your eBook.

#90

Write Another Book!

How many books did you write so far? If you only have one book, it's time to consider writing another book. A book series is an excellent way to market books. Planning a book series ahead of time is also a great way to tell the world about all your upcoming books. Once you finish your second and third books, etc., remember to place an image of the other books in your series in the back of each book.

#91

Have a Raffle

For my children's books, which are all related to cooking and baking, I purchased a few kitchen-themed items including children's aprons, plastic cooking utensils, oven mitts and chef's hats and I created a gift basket to raffle off at an in-person book event. Depending on how much you spend on the items for your raffle, you can decide if raffle tickets will be free or if you want to charge a certain amount. You can purchase a roll of raffle tickets at the dollar store as well. I have tried this several times, mostly with free entrees, but I also tried it by offering raffle tickets for $1.00. I had plenty of takers and earned over $30.00 for a basket of items that cost be $20.00'

You can include anything you like in your gift basket raffle. You don't have to giveaway your book. Instead, you can give away items related to your book as an incentive for readers to buy your book.

#92

Create a Poll

To engage with your audience, you can create a poll on social media such as Facebook or LinkedIn. If your book is nonfiction, I would recommend creating a poll on LinkedIn for business topics. Facebook can be used for different genres and some groups on Facebook may allow you to post a poll.

The objective of creating a poll is to increase engagement with your audience. The poll should be a question related to your book in some way. For fiction, pique their interest by asking them something about the character in your book. For nonfiction, ask a question related to a tip you can offer from your book.

#93

Create a Quiz

Similar to a poll, a quiz could be something you can create as a downloadable file. You also create an interactive quiz using an app. Consider creating a quiz about your book and give entrants incentive to enter by offering them a prize if they complete the quiz. The prize can be a free chapter of your book!

#94

Enter a Contest

There are a ton of contests online which offer book promotion, banners, seals and more. Be careful not to spend too much time and money on contests, especially the ones which charge a fee. Although I have tried to enter several contests as an experiment, including free ones and fee-based contests, I usually avoid them altogether. Most of them are a lot of hype without any long-term gain, although there are exceptions. For example, some websites will offer an electronic image of a banner for the top 3 winners, which you can proudly display on your website or marketing materials. This might cause someone to look at your book a second time and decide to purchase it based on an award or banner. However, if the company providing the award isn't very prestigious, although the banner might be attractive, it may not result in a major sales boost, long-term sales. or much notoriety.

The other consideration is the time it will take you to enter, promote and track the activity while the contest is taking place. Even if you only spend 15 minutes each day checking activity, monitoring stats, and posting shameless plugs asking for votes, that hour or whatever time spent could be spent more wisely, working on other types of book marketing. Here is an example of an announcement I posted when I entered a content for one of my non-fiction software training books:

> 📚 📖VOTE *** VOTE *** VOTE 📖 📚

> Please vote for my latest book, Microsoft Excel Tips, Tricks and Shortcuts: Learn Formulas, Functions and Formatting in 20 Mini-Lessons, via the link below, click on right arrow and go to the Business category, scroll down to

find my book, click once to vote, many thanks!!!!! P.S. remember today is the last day that the e-book version of my Excel book is free on Amazon.

Conclusion: If you must enter contests, try free contests or ones that do not require an astronomical amount of money and time. If you win a book contest, by all means, share the news all over your social media and post the winning banner on your marketing materials. LinkedIn has a section called *Accomplishments* where you can post Honors and Awards on your profile.

#95

Order Business Cards

This is an old school marketing method, but it comes in handy at in-person events. Business cards can easily be created online using tools like Canva, which offers a variety of business card templates. You can also use websites such as Vista Print to design and order business cards. This is less expensive that hiring someone to design and create your cards. Consider including an image of your book on the front or back of the card. Include your bio and where someone can purchase your book.

#96

Order Bookmarks

Bookmarks are a hot item to give away at book events. Like business cards, you can design and order a batch of bookmarks easily using online templates, also available on Canva. Showcase your book cover, a little about your book and a link to your book page on your bookmark!

Orders Mugs, T-Shirts or Pens

Have your considered ordering other merchandise to promote your book? This does require a bit more of an investment, but it can be another lead magnet for your book or book series. Imagine your character on a mug or T-shirt. Pens are limited for space, but you can order pens which include your name and author website. You can sell this merchandise online or in person or consider including giving away some items in your raffle gift basket!

#98

Purchase a Retractable Banner

For in-person author events and festivals, you can order a retractable banner for your table. These can range in price from $65 to well over $100. You can showcase your book and logo on your banner and display it all in-person events, as well as online events as well. It can also be used as a background when recording videos about your book.

#99

Use Food or Other Props

Is your book about food? Why not consider having an artificial replica of your food item? For example, one of my children's books is about an apple cake. I found someone who Instagram who makes artificial cakes in all shapes and sizes. I contacted her and sent her a picture of my children's book cover and ideas for a faux cake to display. I bring the faux cake to all my in-person events for the display table.

If you have a children's book, you can buy or make related props for your display table or to give out for free. I like to give out free gifts to all my customers. Since my children's books are about cooking and recipes, I bought a couple dozen aprons at the dollar store. I also bought a pack of squishy apples to give out as a free gift.

If your books are nonfiction, consider other props related to your book. For my computer books, I bring a computer ornament for the display table. I also bought a bunch of mini notebooks to give out for free. The mini notebooks were so popular, and people wanted to buy them, so I started selling those as well as!

Whatever your book is about, I guarantee that there is a prop or gift related to your book that you can give away or use as a promotional prop on your display table. If you are only selling virtual, you can still create a display table or take pictures of your promotional props and include them in your promotional graphics on social media.

#100

Develop a Mascot

Consider creating a mascot for your book. A mascot is a person, animal, or object used as a symbolic figure for your business. It is designed to bring you good luck. If you have a children's book or other fictional book, consider creating a mascot based on your main character or a sidekick character in your book. Bring your main character to life as a digital animation. You can also consider purchasing a plush figure for display purposes.

If your book is nonfiction, perhaps you can create a mascot for the object mentioned in your book. Whether it's a computer, car or gardening, the possibilities are endless.

The Most Important Strategy

#101

The Positive Marketing Mindset

Although you might not think of meditating and have the right mindset as forms of marketing, they are absolutely some of the most important habits to practice daily. Speak in a positive tone as well. Here are some examples of how to turn worrisome or negative thinking into positive thinking:

Negative Mindset: *"I haven't sold any books yet, and I'm not sure what I'm doing wrong."*
Positive Mindset: *"My goal is to sell at least 25 books today, and I'm going to do everything I can to make that happen."*

Negative Mindset: *"Can you believe after all the work I've done on my book, someone told me I would never sell any books."*
Positive Mindset: *"I got a negative comment today, but I'm not going to let it get to me. If anything, it will make me work harder to sell more books."*

Negative Mindset: *"Someone had the nerve to tell me that my cover was scary and too confusing for a children's book."*
Positive Mindset: *"Someone provided some honest feedback about my cover. I'm going to consider making some changes in the future for a possible re-release of my book."*

Acting positive is equally as important. When attending a book event, whether in-person or online, make the most of each situation. Hold your head high and be proud of the author you have become! Focus on the positive and achieving your goals. Be grateful and thankful for a successful book launch, a profitable author event and increasing monthly sales.

Surround yourself with positive people and entrepreneurs. Smile and greet every single customer with a friendly hello. Try to make eye contact with visitors. Engage in conversation. Thinking positive, acting positive and envisioning a successful outcome makes a world of difference.

Other Expensive Alternatives

If your budget will allow, here are several additional expensive marketing options to consider:

- **Hire a Marketing Expert** – Do your research and find a marketing expert who can help you with your marketing strategies. LinkedIn is a good place to start when looking for professionals. Select someone who has a good track record, ample experience, and most importantly, pick someone who is familiar with your particular genre.

- **Purchase a Masterclass on Book Marketing** – There are thousands of masterclasses offered and the list continues to increase. If you have explored YouTube videos already and need something more expensive and organized, look into a masterclass on book marketing. Same as a marketing expert, you want to find a course which is geared towards your type of book and one which will meet your goals.

- **Purchase a Cameo from a Celebrity** – Have you heard of Cameo? It's an ongoing trend to have a celebrity talk about your book. Just go to cameo.com for more information. Should you have Snoop Dogg talk about your book? Is it wise to invest in a small fortune to have someone from the Harry Potter series mention your book? It depends on your budget, if it's a good match, and most important, where you will be sharing the video. It could generate a lot of likes and comments, but will it convert to sales? Results may vary and be different for each person and each book.

Do's and Don'ts

- Don't Do Book Review Swaps – I know it's tempting, but the idea of "Hey, I'll review your book if you review mine" isn't really a strategy. It's a desperate form of begging for a review. Yes, we have all either done it once or twice (me included) but it's very risky. Amazon has a way of tracking these things and may take down your reviews if they see a pattern of book review swaps.
- Don't make it all about the money. Yes, it's true – money makes the world go 'round, and unfortunately, everything boils down to money. However, focusing *only* on money and how much money you will make can set you up for disappointment. Focus first on giving...what can you give to the world? Then focus on your earnings. Build your brand and your book following and then the money will come!
- Don't design your book cover if you have zero graphic design experience.
- Don't try to do everything yourself thinking you will save money and still earn big royalties.
- Don't not do marketing – in other words, it's important to do some marketing. The more you market, the better the chance your sales will increase.

Conclusion

Why does a book sell?

- It is unique.
- It solves a problem.
- It contains information that people are interested in, but it is presented in an exceptional way.
- It is entertaining.
- It evokes emotion.
- Readers trust the information presented in your book because you have established authority in your field.
- You have convinced others to purchase your book by demonstrating how your book has affected others in a positive way.
- You have lots of good, honest reviews.
- Your book has an awesome, beautiful cover, and it is appropriate for its genre.
- Your book title is on-point – it is trendy and search-friendly (nonfiction), attractive and catchy (fiction) or adorable/cute (children's books).
- Your book description has been optimized with search-friendly copy.
- Your book has excellent rankings and has achieved the #1 New Release banner and/or the #1 Best Seller banner on Amazon.
- You are popular and have an increasing, respectable following.

I'll leave you with final question:

If your book is idle, what can you do – what can you change, to make it better?

Resources

Email Marketing Options

https://mailchimp.com/pricing/marketing

https://www.aweber.com/pricing-t2.htm

https://www.mailerlite.com/pricing

https://www.constantcontact.com/pricing

https://convertkit.com/pricing

Free Logos Creation Tools

https://www.canva.com/logos/templates

https://hatchful.shopify.com

https://www.logomaker.com

Marketing Materials

https://www.vistaprint.com

Canva Training

Click here to watch my free 1-hour tutorial to learn all about Canva:
https://www.youtube.com/hashtag/ezcanva

Canva Sign up

Try Canva Pro for free (I am a Canva partner):

geni.us/getcanva

Amazon Book Ads

https://advertising.amazon.com/solutions/industries/book-ads

https://kdp.amazon.com/en_US/help/topic/G201499010

The Difference Between Boosted Posts and Facebook Ads

https://www.facebook.com/business/help/317083072148603

Instagram Advertising

https://business.instagram.com/advertising

Pinterest Advertising

https://business.pinterest.com/en/

TikTok Advertising

https://www.tiktok.com/business/en-US

LinkedIn Advertising

https://business.linkedin.com/marketing-solutions/ads

Other Publishing Platforms for eBooks (for Perma-Free Books):

Draft2Digital: https://www.draft2digital.com

Smashwords: https://www.smashwords.com

The Author Journey Success Toolkit

More Books in the Series to Help You Along Your Journey

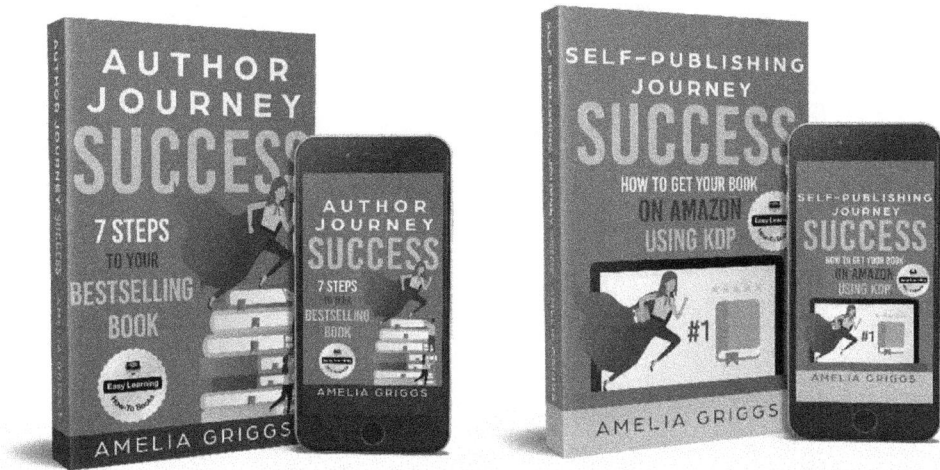

Get the Companion Workbook
Large 8 ½ X 11 Size Worksheets

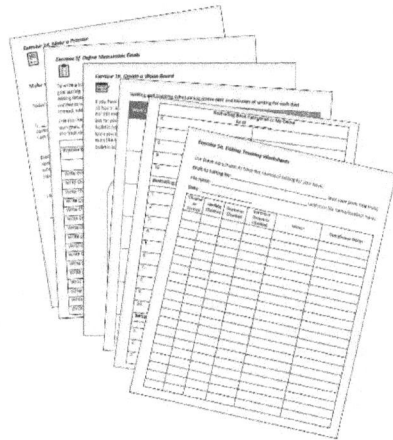

www.ameliaswritingcorner.com/toolkit

geni.us/authoramelia

How did you like this book?

Can you let me know what you found the most helpful in this book?

I understand that you may have purchased this book online or in a bookstore, so there are several ways that you can help. If you purchased the book online, you could leave a review on the website where you purchased the book. Online reviews help online rankings, which customers look for when they decide to make a purchase. If you purchased the book in a bookstore, consider letting the bookstore know how much you enjoyed the book. Reviews and feedback are so important and will truly help me provide more books like this one!

If you purchased this book on Amazon, here's how to post a review:

1. Go to the product detail page for the item.
2. Click *Write a customer review* in the *Customer Reviews* section. To get to the *Customer Reviews* section, click on existing reviews, or scroll down towards the bottom of the product page, and look for *Review this product*; then click Write a customer review. If you've placed an order for the item, you can also go to *Your Orders* and click *Write a product review*.
3. Select a Star Rating. A green check mark shows for successfully submitted ratings.
4. (Optional) Add photos, headline, or comments and click *Submit*.

Follow me on Instagram by searching for @ameliagwrites or go to:

www.instagram.com/ameliagwrites

View all my books here:

geni.us/authoramelia

Thank you in advance for your feedback!

Amelia

Other Business Books by Amelia Griggs

Microsoft Office How-To Book and Video Series:

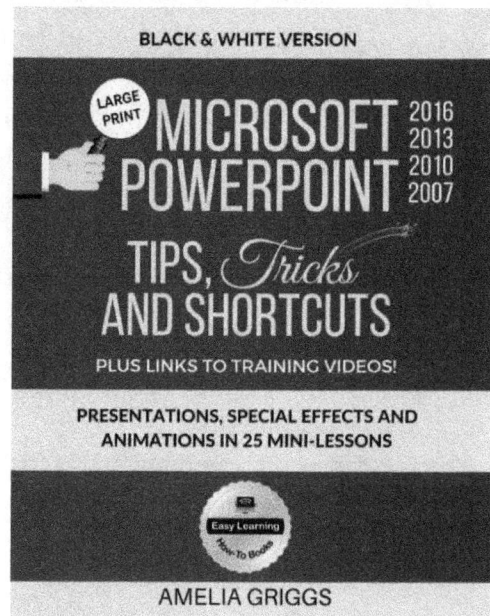

SECOND EDITION

MICROSOFT WORD 2016 2013 2010 2007

TIPS, *Tricks* AND SHORTCUTS

PLUS LINKS TO TRAINING VIDEOS!

35 MINI-LESSONS TO WORK SMARTER, SAVE TIME, AND INCREASE PRODUCTIVITY

Easy Learning How-To Books

AMELIA GRIGGS

MICROSOFT EXCEL 2016 2013 2010 2007

TIPS, *Tricks* AND SHORTCUTS

PLUS LINKS TO TRAINING VIDEOS!

LEARN FORMULAS, FUNCTIONS AND FORMATTING IN 20 MINI-LESSONS

Easy Learning How-To Books

AMELIA GRIGGS

MICROSOFT POWERPOINT 2016 2013 2010 2007

TIPS, *Tricks* AND SHORTCUTS

PLUS LINKS TO TRAINING VIDEOS!

PRESENTATIONS, SPECIAL EFFECTS AND ANIMATIONS IN 25 MINI-LESSONS

Easy Learning How-To Books

AMELIA GRIGGS

BLACK & WHITE VERSION

LARGE PRINT **MICROSOFT POWERPOINT** 2016 2013 2010 2007

TIPS, *Tricks* AND SHORTCUTS

PLUS LINKS TO TRAINING VIDEOS!

PRESENTATIONS, SPECIAL EFFECTS AND ANIMATIONS IN 25 MINI-LESSONS

Easy Learning How-To Books

AMELIA GRIGGS

geni.us/authoramelia

Children's Books by Amelia Griggs

Bella and Mia Adventure Series:

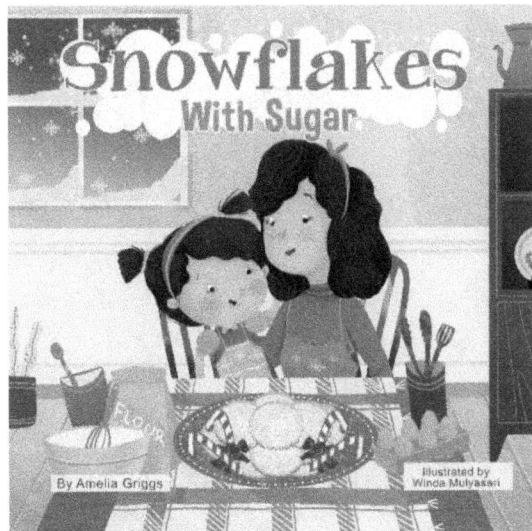

geni.us/authoramelia

Other Books by Amelia Griggs

Bella and Friends Learning Series:

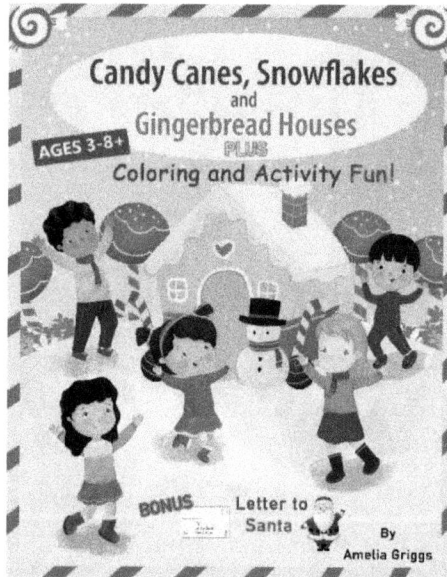

geni.us/authoramelia

www.ingramcontent.com/pod-product-compliance
Lightning Source LLC
Chambersburg PA
CBHW051416200326
41520CB00023B/7254